MAKING WORDS STICK

Strategies that build vocabulary and reading comprehension in the elementary grades

KELLIE BUIS

Pembroke Publishers Limited

Dedication
To those who are intrigued and inspired by the words

Acknowledgements

A profound thanks to...

...my mother and father for their gift of words

...my husband John, for having the best stories of all

...my children, for their support and encouragement

...Colin Chow, for his extraordinary teaching partnership

...the members of Lom Cira, for their tireless work with literacy

...the members of the SFU team, for their dedication to best practice

© 2004 Pembroke Publishers
538 Hood Road
Markham, Ontario, Canada L3R 3K9
www.pembrokepublishers.com

Distributed in the U.S. by Stenhouse Publishers
P.O. Box 11020
Portland, ME 04101
www.stenhouse.com

We acknowledge the financial support of the Government of Canada through the Book Publishing Industry Development Program (BPIDP) for our publishing activities.

We acknowledge the Government of Ontario through the Ontario Media Development Corporation's Ontario Book Initiative.

Library and Archives Canada Cataloguing in Publication

Buis, Kellie
   Making words stick : strategies that build vocabulary and reading comprehension in the elementary grades / Kellie Buis.

Includes index.
For use in grades K-8.
ISBN 1-55138-174-5

   1. Vocabulary—Study and teaching (Elementary) 2. Reading comprehension—Study and teaching (Elementary) I. Title. II. Series: Teaching strategies

LB1574.5.B83 2004   372.44   C2004-903661-0

Editor: Kat Mototsune
Cover Design: John Zehethofer
Cover Photography: Ajay Photographics, Alexander Simone
Typesetting: Jay Tee Graphics Ltd.

Printed and bound in Canada
9 8 7 6 5 4 3 2 1

Table of Contents

Introduction

Research on vocabulary instruction is clear. There is a strong correlation between vocabulary knowledge and reading comprehension (The National Reading Panel document on teaching children to read, 2000). When words stick in the minds of young readers, the readers better understand the text. This book provides elementary teachers with a specific system of best-practice vocabulary instruction that will make oral and printed vocabulary stick.

Some children come to school rich with behaviors of what good readers do, and fat with stores of usable vocabulary. Others come to school in a state of "word poverty" (Moats, 2001), poor in terms of their understanding of what good readers do and showing huge deficits in their meaningful and memorable vocabulary. Literacy researcher Moats advises that this word poverty is most prevalent in ESL students from minority groups, and students from low socioeconomic backgrounds.

The good news is that shortcomings in word knowledge don't usually signify a cognitive deficit but typically reflect the child's level of word experience and instruction. Biemiller assures us that sound vocabulary instruction can teach students the words they need to learn to read (Beck, Perfetti, & McKeown, 1982; Biemiller, 2001). Other researchers confirm that we make words stick through experience and instruction (Allen, 1999).

The bad news is that, despite a long history of research correlating word knowledge and reading comprehension, there is limited translation of this into classroom practice. Many teachers devote little time to vocabulary instruction (Scott, Jamieson & Asselin, 2003), or those who devote time to vocabulary instruction typically use strategies that do not improve students' vocabulary and comprehension abilities (2002, Nagy, 1988). Janet Allen (1999) suggests, "vocabulary is one of those educational arenas in which research and best practice are elusive." Even with the resurgence of interest in vocabulary development as part of many school-district literacy initiatives, there remains little evidence that effective methods of vocabulary instruction, grounded in research, are being used by elementary teachers today (Blachowicz and Fisher, 2004).

More than ever, teachers need practical knowledge of a specific system of best-practice vocabulary instruction to help make words stick in the minds of young readers. *Making Words Stick* synthesizes research into a system of consistent, anchored vocabulary experiences teachers can use to anchor students' vocabulary and improve their reading comprehension. Set in the familiar language-learning contexts of read-alouds, shared reading, and centres, this plan provides multiple opportunities for explicit, mediated instruction in vocabulary throughout the school day. It can make vocabulary stick for even the most diverse, challenging groups of learners, especially those from low socioeconomic or ESL backgrounds.

Chapter 1 introduces the system of instructional strategies of semantic mapping, prompting conversations with STRETCH charts, and independent word play. It conceptualizes the plan of vocabulary instruction and outlines the accomplishments that can be made.

Chapter 2 introduces teachers to the explicit teaching of semantic mapping. Chapter 3 presents, in practical terms, the method to deliver this strategy. Research informs us that there is a great need for the explicit teaching of new vocabulary to students (Blachowicz and Fisher, 2004).

Chapter 4 introduces the use of STRETCH charts. Chapter 5 presents the practical application of the STRETCH-chart strategy in guiding students' talk about text to further expand their knowledge of words and reading strategies. Research informs us that we need to help students build strategies to learn new words independently (Blachowicz and Fisher, 2004).

Chapter 6 introduces the use of centres to situate the strategy for independent word play. Chapter 7 presents collections of engaging and effective centre activities to develop the students' awareness and love of words. Researchers advise us that we need to encourage students to play with and explore words (Blachowicz and Fisher, 2004).

Making Words Stick answers many of the questions teachers ask about the most effective methods to deepen and enrich the word knowledge of our fledgling literacy learners. Use it as a resource to answer commonly asked questions about vocabulary instruction:

- How many words can I teach in a lesson? In a week? In a year?
- What words should I teach?
- How many experiences will be necessary before new vocabulary sticks?
- How can I most effectively teach vocabulary during read-alouds, shared reading, guided reading, and independent centre time?
- What are the most effective and manageable teaching strategies for instruction in vocabulary to deepen and enrich language learning?

This book has been produced specifically for two groups of educators. One group consists of pre-service and beginning teachers who are in the formative stage of developing their beliefs and understandings of methods for instruction in vocabulary. It is especially useful if they work with ESL students from minority groups or students from low socioeconomic backgrounds. The other group consists of practising teachers at various levels of education — including classroom teaching, resource room teaching, curriculum/instructional development, and evaluation of curriculum — who are looking to make changes in their current vocabulary teaching practices. It is useful for teachers who want to move away from a method of "assign, define, and test" and shift their practice toward a concept-based, multi-layered knowledge of words, but who simply haven't known how to do it … until now.

Chapter 1: Anchoring Word Knowledge

A word is not a crystal, transparent and unchanging, it is the skin
of a living thought and may vary greatly in color and content
according to the circumstances and time in which it is used.
—Oliver Wendell Holmes, Jr. (1843–1935)

Research instructs us that students need a more comprehensive, deeper
conceptual understanding of words. Anchored vocabulary instruction
assists our students in holding on to this deeper conceptual understanding (Juel & Deffes, 2004). We use an explicit, systematic, and
extensive system of vocabulary instruction to anchor our students' full-
concept knowledge of words. We use it to make words stick.

Semantic mapping, STRETCH charts, and independent word play
are the three research-based, best-practice strategies we use in this plan
to secure complex word knowledge. We specifically and consistently
use these three strategies, one after another, to give our students repeated exposure to a set of target words. Here we have the integration of
key words during semantic mapping, repetition of them during
STRETCH-chart prompted conversations, and assimilation and transfer of them into independent use during word play. We use this system
to provide rich, routine opportunities for multi-layered contact with
key vocabulary. It helps our students build word-concept
knowledge beyond memorizing straight definitions. Instead, they build
multi-dimensional concept-based meaning for words that can be used
in different contexts and applied to their own lives.

In anchoring specific word learning recurrently and consistently
throughout the day, we create a broader vocabulary program than is
being used in many classrooms (Graves, 2000; Graves & Watts-Taffe,
2002). We ensure that more words go into our students' lexicons.
Biemiller reminds us that "developing a comprehensive understanding
of a word comes through repeated exposure to the word in a variety of
rich contexts" (2000b). With this expansive vocabulary program we can
make words stick.

Strategies for Making Words Stick
1. Semantic Mapping
2. STRETCH-chart Prompted
   Conversations
3. Independent Word Play

Levels of Understanding

Many of our fledgling readers do not learn vocabulary at a deep
conceptual level by just reading or by being given brief contextual definitions. Few texts are written in a manner that allows students to walk

through them and obtain more than the incidental, single-meaning understandings of the words. Research-based guiding principles about vocabulary instruction confirm that word knowledge is complex and consists of more than knowing definitions (Scott, Jamieson & Asselin, 2003). Methods to learn new vocabulary through definitions, contexts, and word study can provide some information about the meaning of a word, but each of these methods of instruction alone has significant limitations. Students, especially language-disadvantaged students, need more than a linear, left-to-right method of processing text or context-based definitions to deepen their understanding of it.

To anchor our students with a deeper conceptual understanding of words and optimal reading comprehension, we use each strategy and context to guide their attention to word components, letters, and sounds (graphophonics), word meanings (semantics), and the relationships between words (syntax). This knowledge may include students' familiarity with a word's *polysemy*, or multiple meanings, and its *morphology*, or derivation (Nagy & Scott, 2000; Nation, 1990).

A full-concept level of word knowledge is attained when students learn about word families, the multiple meanings of words, ways to extend them into meaningful use, ways to discriminate them from similar words, and ways to integrate them comfortably into their own use (Allen, 1999). Word knowledge can be broken down into three levels:

Three Levels of Understanding
Verbal Association
Partial Concept
Full Concept

Verbal-Association Level
Low level of understanding through context clues in reading:
- everyday reading
- definitions
- single contextual meaning
- interactive reading

Partial-Concept Level
Moderate level of understanding through individual play to increased word knowledge:
- work with multiple meanings
- work with explicit strategies to learn words
- work with graphic organizers to extend definitions and nuances of words

Full-Concept Level
High level of understanding through visual presentation of rich knowledge of the shape/structure, sound, word families, and multiple meanings or nuances of words:
- play with word families
- play with multiple meanings
- extend definitions
- discriminate words from similar words
- play with explicit strategies for connecting/extending words
- integrate words into meaningful use

Students typically attain a partial-concept level or the full-concept knowledge (Baker, Simon & Kameenui, 1995a) of key words with the semantic mapping strategy.

Students typically attain partial-concept level when they use STRETCH charts to prompt their talk about the words. They learn a deeper level of understanding of the words through conversation than they would if they just read them. Students can also attain a full-concept knowledge using STRETCH charts.

Students typically attain only verbal-association level (Baker, Simon & Kameenui, 1995a) when they read alone or in a small group during centres. They may attain partial-concept or full-concept understanding when they anchor their new word knowledge through independent word play.

Cycle of Anchored Vocabulary Instruction

This explicit, systematic, and extensive plan of vocabulary instruction gives students at least eight to ten systematic passes to anchor the vocabulary learning of between six and eight key words each few days. By the end of this specific and consistent cycle of vocabulary instruction, students will typically develop a level of understanding of four to six target words, including all kinds of information about them: related word-family members, multiple meanings, ways to extend the meaning, ways to discriminate the word from similar words, and ways to integrate the word into personal use.

When we use this coherent plan of semantic mapping, STRETCH charts, and independent word play with students, we are able to anchor a higher level of word knowledge for each of the key words. We give students exposure to more knowledge of the words with each strategy and context used. Word knowledge is complex, and students require many meaningful and memorable passes at it to anchor it in their minds.

Vocabulary Instruction Contexts

We best anchor students' vocabulary learning by engaging them with semantic mapping, STRETCH charts, and independent word-play strategies within three familiar, common-practice, language-learning contexts — read-aloud, shared reading, and independent centres. Our students anchor their word knowledge by participating in semantic mapping during a read-aloud, STRETCH-chart prompted conversations during shared reading, and independent word play during centres. The language-rich environments can be conceptualized as "to" (read-aloud), "with" (shared reading), and "by" (independent centres) spheres to anchor vocabulary learning (Mooney, 1990).

Semantic Mapping

We most often begin the process of anchoring important words before we share the read-aloud or view the picture. We begin with a poster-size

The read-aloud/picture study context is characterized as a "to" reading context, where we read or teach a picture study "to" the students. We use our semantic mapping strategy to introduce new important vocabulary "to" them.

semantic map, with the topic in the middle and the four to six key words that we will anchor branching out. We access the students' background knowledge by asking them what they already know about the words. We add the students' prior knowledge to the map. This semantic map captures the "big picture" display of what they already know about the new words being learned. Conjuring up this information with the students gives them a context in which the learning is not entirely new or overwhelming to them. It reassures them of what they already know. We then build on this prior knowledge, adding the new ideas we have collected from the read-aloud and/or picture study.

Accomplishments

During the semantic mapping strategy we

- implement a read "to" context
- provide a visual display of the topic and the important 4–6 key concept words
- activate the students' prior knowledge of these key words; record these on the semantic map
- explicitly provide definitional and contextual information about the key words
- explicitly teach pragmatics (relationship between text and content), semantics (meaning vocabulary), syntax (grammar), and graphophonics (conventions of print) of these key words
- use the read-aloud and/or picture study to develop the key words
- draw attention once again to the pragmatics (relationship between text and content), semantics (meaning vocabulary), syntax (grammar), and graphophonics (conventions of print) of these words
- draw attention to words selected by the students
- assess and evaluate student progress and performance with new word knowledge

STRETCH Charts and Shared Reading

In the reading "with" context, we cultivate talk about the text "with" the students' through STRETCH-chart prompted conversations.

This second pass at key vocabulary comes through prompted conversations about a shared reading text. We further anchor the conceptual understanding of new word knowledge by using a set of conversation prompts, STRETCH charts, to guide students' talk "with" a collaborative discourse community. The students review and discover additional meanings of the key words and many other words in the shared reading text through this social, collaborative, and active conversation. We cultivate a high level of consciousness of all the aspects of word knowledge — the pragmatics or relationship between the text and the content, semantics, syntax, and graphophonics — through these prompted conversations. We code the text with colored highlighters as part of the strategy to touch the words and connect new knowledge with any prior knowledge. We add the words they are talking about to the Word Wall to engage students in the active analysis of words.

Accomplishments

During the STRETCH chart strategy we

- read "with" the students
- provide STRETCH charts as a discourse organizer to provide engaged, active analysis of words
- model ways to introduce a text
- read the text together
- share responsibility with students for discussion of some of the definitional and contextual information of the text
- use the shared reading "talk about text" to call students' attention to important key, concept, common, high-frequency, personal, and utility words
- guide the talk about the pragmatics, semantics, syntax, and graphophonics of the text
- guide the "talk about text" to call students' attention to important strategies good readers and writers use
- highlight/code the STRETCH-chart words, phrases, and sentences on the page of text
- add the highlighted/coded STRETCH-chart words to the Word Wall for future reference
- review and/or list on chart paper the strategies that good readers and writers use
- assess and evaluate student progress and performance

Independent Word Play During Centres

In the "by" context of independent word play, we nurture students' "ways of being" individuals reading, writing, and playing with words "by" themselves.

This final pass at key vocabulary learning comes through students reading, writing, representing, and playing with words during independent centres. The students review and discover additional word meanings and nuances of vocabulary. During this differentiated learning time, we nurture their independent "ways of being" good readers and writers, and meet their specific language needs.

With this final context of our broad-based word-study plan, new important words can be once again viewed, spoken, and played with "by" our students.

Accomplishments

During the independent word play we

- have students read in a "by" context — by themselves, or in a small group
- implement reading, writing, representing, and word centres to further anchor their knowledge of important concept, common, high-frequency, utility, and personal words
- provide opportunities for students to integrate word and concept into meaningful use
- provide opportunities for connecting and extending words
- provide opportunities to discriminate words from similar words
- provide opportunities to work/play with word families, multiple meanings
- host reading and writing conferences with individual students

- monitor and reinforce the independent play/practice of the students with reading and writing strategies
- use this time for students to participate in recreational choice reading and writing to learn words as they appear in context
- assess and evaluate individual student reading and writing progress and performance

We anchor the rich development of vocabulary for our most at-risk students with their full immersion in these three vocabulary-learning contexts. This eclectic collection of strategies works effectively as a coherent, cohesive plan to anchor the full-concept knowledge of words for even our most language-disadvantaged students. Our students will typically develop a deeper level of conceptual knowledge of key words through their continual revising and revisiting of word meanings (semantics), grammar (syntax), conventions of print (graphophonics), and genre (pragmatics) through each of these contexts. Anchoring new word knowledge through multiple strategies and contexts improves our chances of meeting the needs of both our language-advantaged and language-disadvantaged students.

Conceptualizing Strategies

The strategies we use to anchor word knowledge at a deeper level of understanding can be conceptualized in numerous ways. They are each characterized by the use of different literacy contexts, modes of communication, and methods to deliver vocabulary instruction. They demand different levels of understanding, teacher support, groupings, number, and kinds of words studied.

Although each strategy is somewhat unique, the one common thread running through each is their role as anchors for the full conceptual meaning of the same target words.

Modes of Communication

We anchor students' deeper knowledge of words with a program balanced in the use of visual, oral, and written modes of communication. We nurture this deeper knowledge by first creating a context of visual communication with large, colorful semantic maps of important words from a read-aloud or picture study. We then nurture word knowledge by creating a context that attends to oral communication with lively, student-centred, whole-group, STRETCH-chart prompted conversations about a shared text. We further nurture word knowledge by creating a context for independent practice of visual, oral, and written communication. We create a balance between each of these communication styles to meet the needs of our diverse groups of learners.

Types of Instruction

Each of these word-anchoring strategies has a particular level of instruction associated with it. Semantic mapping requires a high level of explicit, direct instruction by the teacher. STRETCH-chart prompted conversations require the students to take more responsibility for learning through their active participation in conversations about their growing word knowledge. Independent word-play centres are largely student-centred with low-level instructional support; the exception is the guided reading centre that, like read-alouds, has a high level of instruction. We need a variety of strategies and levels of teaching support to effectively anchor word understanding of our linguistically advantaged and disadvantaged students.

Number of Words

There are approximately 88,000 word families in English (Nagy and Anderson, 1985). Most of these words are so rare that they are almost never encountered in a lifetime.

Each of these word-anchoring strategies teaches the same number of key words. However, each has an additional number and type of words that may be taught and learned to a verbal-association, partial-concept, or full-concept level (Baker, Simon & Kameenui, 1995a).

If students accumulate about 3,000 to 4,000 words per year, it would be unrealistic to teach the meaning of each of these words. We do have some guidelines of the numbers of words our students should be exposed to. James Flood, noted vocabulary researcher from San Diego State University, informs us that it is sufficient to cultivate knowledge of about five words per lesson (Brassel & Flood, 2004) and about 400 per year (Beck et al, 2002). For the purposes of this system of vocabulary instruction, repeated exposure to four to six words throughout these three contexts would anchor a healthy store of over 800 words for our students. We extend the learning of these four to six words over the contexts so that students encounter at least eight to ten exposures to each new word, the estimated number for it to become part of their lexicon — for it to stick (Nagy & Scott, 2000; Beck et al, 2000). If we can make good sense of five words per literacy lesson, and anchor them through the three vocabulary learning contexts, and we do this three times per week, our students will typically learn more than five hundred words at a deep conceptual level in a school year — 5 key words x 3 times per week x 35 weeks = 525 words per school year.

Children know about 8,000 common words (Brassell & Flood, 2004).

Kinds of Words

There are many excellent sources for lists of words on the Internet. Students can be challenged to access this information as part of their shared responsibility for the learning of words.

There are a number of kinds of words we work with throughout the year with each strategy. Students need basic sight words, high-frequency words, utility words, and words found in their school readings and in their own personal reading and writing. They need to learn high-frequency words at their reading level. They need to learn some utility words, the words they encounter less frequently. They also need new concept and content/topic words. We need to teach the content-area words that are associated with math, social studies, or sciences. They also require knowledge of some literary words.

Groupings

Group sizes change with the kind of instructional strategies we are working with. We use holistic semantic mapping to anchor new important vocabulary inclusively, into the existing stores of vocabulary of all students. Use of STRETCH charts can include all students in the prompted conversation about their knowledge of words, or we divide them up into smaller groups to participate in their talk about text. With independent word play, we have students work with vocabulary on their own, in partnerships, or in small groups to develop their own particular meaningful use of the vocabulary.

Modes of Learning

We anchor student's deeper knowledge of words with a program balanced in the use of strategies that focus on different modes of learning (visual, auditory, tactile, etc.). We need to be cognizant of a variety of learning-style preferences if all of our students are to make sense of new words in their own unique ways. We meet the diverse learning needs of our students when we strategically plan a variety of activities to match and sometimes stretch their various cognitive styles.

We know that not all students process text most effectively in a linear, left-to-right manner. For many students this way of making sense of information may be foreign and leaves them at a disadvantage. As part of our initiative to meet the diverse needs of our students, we provide activities that match those students who do not learn as effectively with the linear left-to-right orientation. We provide opportunities for them to participate in activities, such a semantic mapping, in which they work with the whole big picture of visual information. This activity requires holistic learning, unlike the parts-to-the-whole style characterized in the linear presentation of STRETCH-chart prompted conversations.

We spend some time making meaning through linear left-to-right text reading, and some time in non-linear guided semantic mapping. We also provide opportunities for students to consolidate their growing word knowledge through a range of styles during the independent centres. As we take our students through the three contexts each day, we use a number of cognitive strategies with them.

Word Anchoring Processes

The strategies for word anchoring explore the different processes involved in word use — integration, repetition, and meaningful use of vocabulary. Explicit semantic mapping demonstrates the integration of new vocabulary. STRETCH-chart prompted conversations involve repeating new key words in context. Independent word play explores the meaningful use of the different aspects of new word use.

All three processes contribute to students' understanding of the different aspects of word use, such as semantics, syntax, graphophonics, and pragmatics.

Semantics (meaning vocabulary)
- word meanings, phrases, sentences, discourse, and whole texts
- multiple meanings
- ideas
- idioms, etc.

Syntax (grammar; relationship between words)
- pattern of sentences, clauses and phrases
- sentence structure
- use of linking words
- paragraphing
- discourse structures, etc.

Graphophonics (conventions of print)
- graphic symbols
- letter–sound relationships
- spelling patterns
- directionality
- spacing
- punctuation, etc.

Pragmatics (relationship between text and content)
- registers
- functions
- forms of representation
- genres

Characteristics of Strategies For Vocabulary Learning

	Semantic Mapping	STRETCH Charts	Independent Word Play
Context	Read-aloud/ Picture study	Shared Reading	Centres
Method	Teacher-directed	Shared responsibility for learning	Student-centred
Modes of Comunication	Visual Oral	Visual Oral Written	Visual Oral Written
Type of Instruction	Explicit	Collaborative conversations/ discussions	Differentiated learning
Level of Instructional Support	High	Moderate	Low
Level of Word Knowledge	Full concept	Partial concept	Verbal association

	Semantic Mapping	STRETCH Charts	Independent Word Play
Levels of Understanding	Deep	Partial	Various
Number of Key Words Learned	4–6 words per lesson	4–6 words per lesson	4–6 words per lesson
Kinds of Words	Words related to read-aloud, students' experiences and/or word study	Basic sight, high-frequency, utility, personal interest, concept, and related content words	Personal, content, and high-utility words; and type of words determined by the teacher to meet the vocabulary learning needs of the individual student
Group Size	Whole class	Whole class or small group	Individual, partners, or small group
Modes of Learning	Holistic: visual representations of vocabulary knowledge	Holistic/part-to-whole learning: linear representation of vocabulary knowledge in context	Holistic and part-to-whole learning: independent practice with visual representations of vocabulary and linear representations of vocabulary learning
Processes	Integration and mapping of new key words	Repetition and conversing about new key words	Meaningful use of and play with new key words
Semantics (meaning vocabulary)	Explicitly map out semantics: ideas, words, idioms, etc.	Converse about semantics: ideas, words, idioms, etc.	Independent play with semantics: ideas, words, idioms, etc.
Syntax (relationship between words)	Map out syntax	Converse about syntax	Independent play with syntax
Graphophonics (conventions of print)	Map out graphophonics	Converse about graphophonics	Independent play with graphophonics
Pragmatics (relationship between text and content)	Map out pragmatics	Converse about pragmatics	Independent play with pragmatics

Active Learning

A student's deeper understanding of words is anchored through social and active participation in an explicit, systematic, and extensive system of key vocabulary instruction. We can see how the three studies encompass multiple modes of communication, levels of understanding, representations of learning, levels of teaching support, groupings, numbers, and kinds of words studied. We can also see what can be accomplished with this three-fold array of best practice vocabulary anchoring activities. By following the strategies of semantic mapping, STRETCH-chart prompted conversation, and independent word play, we lead students through the acts of listening, talking, and playing to anchor word instruction, to make the words stick.

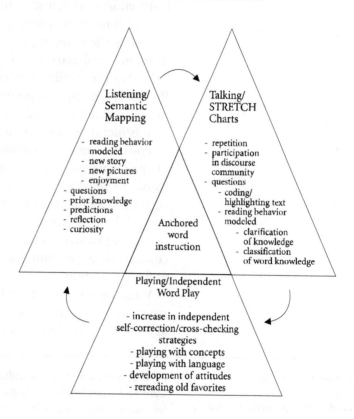

Chapter 2: Semantic Mapping

Reading researchers (Beck, McKeown & Kucan, 2002; Biemiller, 2001b; Nagy, 1988) caution us that vocabulary instruction must be more substantial for words to really stick. Direct, active, and analytical vocabulary instruction is a more effective method to promote learning than instruction in which students only relate words to their own experience or hear context mentioning of definitions (Beck and McKeown, 2001). The semantic mapping strategy is one of the most effective methods to promote vocabulary learning beyond context-mentioned definitions.

Within the familiar context of the read-aloud of our Language Arts Program, semantic mapping begins the process of anchoring students' full conceptual knowledge of words. Semantic mapping of read-alouds/picture studies is the first step in a consistent, explicit, and extensive system of vocabulary instruction, in a whole-to-parts method of anchoring vocabulary that takes students from the whole text, to words, to word parts. It is a way to capture old and new word knowledge from a context of full texts rather than in isolation. It is the "to" part of the "to," "with," and "by" word experiences of the students. It introduces students to the multiple possibilities for key words through contextualized, memorable, and meaningful strategic instruction before and after reading.

With the semantic mapping strategy, we ensure that children learn new vocabulary and how to read by being read to. Semantic mapping of key words is our first important way to make words stick.

Context: *Read-aloud/Picture Study or Common Experience*
Read-aloud/Picture Study: Scarecrow *by Cynthia Rylant*
Important Concept Words: *borrowed, mammoth, real, witness, wonder*
Strategies: *Visual Displays, Semantic Mapping of a Scarecrow*
Level of Instruction: *Teacher-directed, robust, explicit instruction*
Grouping: *Whole-group language experience.*

I share the stunningly beautiful Cynthia Rylant book *Scarecrow* as my read-aloud/picture study. The book shares the story of the scarecrow who, although he is made of straw and borrowed clothes, appreciates his peaceful, gentle life and the privilege of watching nature at work. Rylant uses casual language with simple grace and pleasing rhythms for this heart-warming picture book. The illustrations are exquisite, in soft, muted autumn shades. The words and illustrations are as glorious as a sun-drenched autumn day.

We have been on a field trip to the pumpkin patch and made some rag-tag scarecrows of our own from borrowed clothing and treasures. We have prepared a Thanksgiving feast to celebrate our harvest from our school garden. We are now ready to begin to tackle a deeper, richer knowledge of the big ideas of our curriculum and some of the words from the story. We will anchor the words *borrowed, mammoth, real, witness*, and *wonder* at a deep concept knowledge level. I will use the book to extend the meaningful vocabulary of my students through each of three contexts: the read-aloud/picture study context, the prompted conversation context, and finally independent centre time.

I have selected the words *witnessing* and *wondering* for my teaching of the big idea. These words are not only slightly ahead of the vocabulary of my seven- and eight-year-olds, but they are central to the concepts I am trying to teach, regarding science and writing as processes of "witnessing" and "wondering."

Anchoring Important Concept Words

I selected this read-aloud/picture study and these concept words so that I can take a first pass at exposing my students to important content vocabulary at a level beyond what they would be able to comfortably read. I am exposing them to a deeper understanding of the big ideas, important learning especially for ESL and at-risk students.

I ask them what they know about scarecrows. I print the word *scarecrow* in the middle of the poster-size blank chart during my wait time, and ask the students to help me build a semantic map of the key words from our topic: *borrowed, mammoth, real, witness, wonder.* We say the words slowly as I point out the letters and stretch the sounds out. I want to activate their prior knowledge of these words before I read the book and show them the illustrations. Our list grows as I scribe their ideas onto the large word map. Many of my students will enjoy the simple challenge of listening for these targeted words when we go on to read the story.

I have added the new concept words as branches off of the central word. I will extend my students' meaningful vocabularies by four to six important words formally through this lesson and throughout the course of the day. I will informally revisit these words from time to time over the course of the school year. We will begin to compile a poster-size list of words so that over the year we can revisit various ones from time to time.

I have selected this book largely because the scarecrow's life in

Cynthia Rylant's book is a metaphor for her own life as a writer. When asked to describe her own writing process, she talked about writing not as something she does at a desk, but rather as something she is part of as she "witnesses" or "notices" what goes on in her life. I want my students to begin to live their lives as writers with a great sense of awareness of witnessing what goes on in their lives — much as the scarecrow does in the story.

If my students can perhaps linger for a bit in one place and live through the experience of the scarecrow, they can learn to linger a bit in their own lives, notice things, and layer them with greater meaning in their writing. If my students can deepen their conceptual knowledge of the words *wonder* and *witness*, perhaps they can benefit from thinking their own "long, slow thoughts" and benefit from their own particular noticings, questionings, witnessings, and wonderings about themselves, each other, and the world. This plan to "linger over life" is an important first step in our conceptual understanding to becoming a writer, scientist, and wordsmith.

Anchoring Word Meanings

At the end of the story I take a few minutes to talk about the book with the students. I point to the word *witness* on the semantic map and ask the students to share ideas of how the scarecrow is a witness to life. I add their ideas to the semantic map as we discuss the book.

- What is a witness and what is he witness to?
- I ask the students if they have ever been a witness to something and if they can use the word "witness" in a sentence. I model this by saying "I was witness to _____."
- I ask them what it looks like when a person is "witness" to something.

- We expand the meaning by trying to finish a sentence: When you witness _____ you _____.

Anchoring Common, Everyday Words

As well as anchoring a deeper word knowledge of the key words, I connect them to other common words that hold personal meaning for the students. I want them to select from the story personal words that they like and are likely to encounter in their day-to-day reading. We add more personal words to the semantic map as well. I ask them for some everyday words they remember, and they come up with *smile, high, birds,* and *straw.* They also include the words *button* and *chat.* We will add the verb *tremble* to the line between the words *wonder* and *sun* ("the sun trembled") at the suggestion of one student. We add the verb *floated* between *wonder* and *cloud* ("the clouds floated"), and the verb *wilted* between *wonder* and *vines* ("the vines wilted") at another suggestion. I am careful to explain the words that go on the lines between words on the semantic map. I show the students how to use lines and arrows to connect important information.

We "shake out" (Calhoun, 1999) other supporting words from the illustrations to add to the main collection on the semantic map. We add *grackles, starlings,* and *jays* to the list of birds; *owls, rabbits, spider,* and *mice* are added at the request of the animal lovers in the class. We shake out the borrowed words *jacket, lapel, hat, suit,* and *pants.* Several students are delighted to add *pumpkins, pie-pan hands,* and *ten-foot-tall.*

The visual display of Scarecrow words begins the process of students representing key words for meaningful use in their own life. We create the semantic map to introduce big ideas in science and writing, to activate prior knowledge of the words, and to distinguish the relationships between old word meanings and new ones.

Mapping Our Word Knowledge

Semantics is the study of the meaning of language. It involves the analysis of words, phrases, sentences, discourse, and whole texts. Semantic mapping includes the graphic displaying or "mapping out" of words, phrases, sentences, discourse, or text in a meaningful way. Here, semantic mapping includes the graphic organizing or mapping out of words, phrases, and sentences as new knowledge in a wide variety of formats. We use semantic mapping as the tool to make sense of our students' prior knowledge of target words and their additional learning from the story we read and/or pictures we study.

These visual displays can take a number of different forms, depending on the key words and genre of the read-aloud/picture study. Sometimes words are added randomly to the map, sometimes they are organized as a flow diagram, pyramid, Venn diagram, or boxed chart.

The collection of semantic maps in Chapter 3 showcases a variety of ways to organize a word, phrase, concept, section of text, or discourse in order to break down new knowledge into steps and increase the students' level of understanding. Even though the mapping strategies may take many forms — charts, boxes, outlines — and have a variety of titles — webs, clusters, networks, graphic organizers — they all involve the creation of a diagram on which the relationships among selected words are arranged to extend students' understanding. Some of the semantic maps involve mapping out information from one semantic map format to another.

Semantic mapping has long been recognized as one of the most effective tools for expanding students' vocabulary (Brassel & Flood, 2004). It is one of the most valuable strategies to help ESL students and at-risk students understand vocabulary and learn to read and write. It is often critical in the word-building phase of content-area learning. Semantic mapping can make vocabulary meaningful and memorable in ways that reading text in a linear left-to-right fashion alone cannot. It can make vocabulary knowledge public. It can make vocabulary concrete in ways that spoken language alone cannot. The techniques of webbing, clustering, or mapping helps students generate nonlinear associations and ideas about words. It assists them in being interested in the words. It allows them to feel connected to the important words, and makes them part of the vocabulary learning process.

We place a high priority for the learning of vocabulary through visual displays of vocabulary from our read-alouds and picture studies. It can be a very creative process for students to holistically represent what they already know. Some of our students' best learning is done visually. We value the natural disposition of many of them to organize information in their heads through visual patterns and spatial relationships. When students are given opportunities to learn through mapping, many of them are better able to make sense of new important concept vocabulary. As we increase the mental imagery we use to display new word concepts, their interest typically increases.

Flow diagrams are particularly useful with non-fiction read-alouds that investigate or explain a process or a cause and effect. They can also map out systems or character relationships. They can map out words or full quotations.

We want our students to have plenty of opportunities to work with read-alouds, picture studies, and semantic maps so that we can provide a strong, memorable hook for their new vocabulary learning. When we combine semantic maps with read alouds and/or picture studies, we have an effective way to anchor the in-depth knowledge of important words.

Activating Prior Knowledge

The semantic map establishes a purpose for sharing the read-aloud or picture study.

We create a powerful vocabulary-learning context when we activate students' prior knowledge before sharing a read-aloud or studying a picture. This is done by simply mapping out a visual display of what they already know about the four to six key words. This process of accessing our students' level of knowledge of targeted vocabulary is the first step in making their words stick.

Semantic mapping of prior word knowledge constructs meaning as a three-part relationship between a linguistic form (the name, symbol), the object it refers to, and the concept or the idea of it. Put a nucleus word, the topic or concept, in the centre of the chart and radiate the key words outwards from it. The important words for students to learn can be written in prior to the lesson or added in front of the students. The students' prior knowledge of the key words will be radiated out from here.

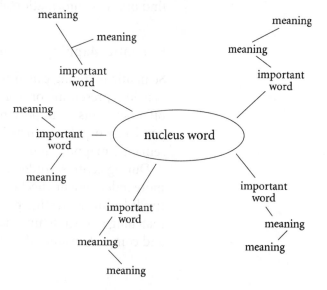

This visual display of what students know helps them begin to make connections to the words or topic of the read-aloud/picture study. The lines and arrows between the information you collect can be inserted before the read-aloud, or added after the read-aloud as another step to make sense of the words. These large-print semantic displays will be completed after the read-aloud.

Access students' prior knowledge by asking them what they know about each of the key words. Encourage them to bring all their knowledge about the topic to the surface before they read, thus setting them into a meaning-based cueing system. This brief guided discussion, lasting two to five minutes, elicits what is collectively known about the key words before reading about them. It prompts the students to realize what personal connections they may already have with the text, and allows them to contemplate the new ones they will make.

- Have students conjure up connections from their previous life experiences, such as what they have read, watched, and done in other places and times.
- Talk about how some of these important words connect to their lives.
- They may have anecdotes that let them share their extended meaning-making of the words.
- Tactile examples of the words can be shared to contribute to the more in-depth knowledge/concept of them.
- Have a student who understands a word volunteer to describe it to the other students.

Encourage all students to anchor their word knowledge from their prior knowledge. Most often, the more accessing of this knowledge they do, the greater the meaning-making that will occur during the read-aloud and when talking about the text. As students listen to the read-aloud, they can see if what they know on the semantic map matches what the text tells them and the pictures show. As they listen, they can find out new information about the words they did not know before.

Semantic Mapping in Centres

Semantic mapping can also be used as a strategy of independent word play in representing or word-play centres (see Chapter 7), where it offers students an important "by" strategy to learn and use in independently organizing new information after the whole-group studies of semantic mapping and the prompted conversations of shared reading.

During centres, students learn semantic mapping strategies that promote independent checking for understanding, nurturing of cooperative learning, activating prior knowledge, improving organization, matching and stretching learning styles, and assisting with vocabulary and comprehension difficulties.

Chapter 3: Using Semantic Mapping

This chapter presents a number of semantic mapping strategies that are suitable for use with the whole class or with small groups in centres. We create a powerful whole-class literacy event or successful centre by challenging students to prepare visual representations of their word knowledge and/or comprehension of a text/picture. For some lessons, invite students to work at a Representing Centre or Word-Play Centre with a semantic map constructed during a read aloud/picture study, and have them independently translate the semantic map into another format for further meaning-making.

Semantic mapping can be used with students in any grade. The difficulty or the complexity lies not in the creation of the visual display itself, but the text or picture used to create it. Semantic mapping can be applied to any genre of read-aloud, picture study, or content information. These strategies can be used with verbal communication, experiential learning, poems, plays, novels, or university texts.

Students with limited word knowledge and reading comprehension benefit from using a variety of mapping formats. In this collection, we have a wide variety of modes and methods to suit and encourage reluctant, linguistically disadvantaged readers, and also to enrich the experience of enthusiastic, linguistically advantaged readers.

With some read-alouds and picture studies, you can expose students to content area materials covering a variety of Language Arts, Science, Social Studies, or Math learning outcomes at one time. This strategy of semantic mapping of key content words is especially useful to teachers who are feeling the pressure to cover a broad number of curriculum topics.

Word Choice

To create the semantic map, first determine the words from the read-aloud or picture study that you want students to learn. Allen (1999) suggests that, in order to teach words at various levels, we need to ask ourselves some questions:

- What words are most important to understanding the text?
- How much prior knowledge will the students have about this word or its related concepts?
- Is the word encountered frequently?
- Does the word have multiple meanings (is it polysemous)?
- Is the concept significant and does it require pre-teaching?
- Which words can be figured out from the context?
- Are there words that could be grouped together to enhance the understanding of a concept?
- What strategies could I employ to help students integrate the word/concept (and related words) into their lives?

- How can I make repeated exposures to the word /concept production and enjoyable?
- How can I help students use the word/concept in meaningful ways in multiple contexts?

Use the form "Choosing Words for Semantic Mapping" on page 25 to explore these questions.

Using a Semantic Map with a Read-aloud/Picture Study

From time to time, you might decide to build maps during (i.e., at the end of a chapter of a novel study) or after reading to help readers make sense of the text, but only if they have already activated their prior knowledge informally.

Once you have selected the key words to learn, prepare a semantic map. For the purposes of new vocabulary development, pre-select the four to six important words, especially those dealing with the "big idea" concept or content, or curriculum-related words.

When creating big visual displays of words, structure the key concept words on the map and then capture the high-interest personal words the students want to "shake out" of the read-aloud/picture study session (Calhoun, 1999). Print the topic word and decide on the arrangement of the four to six branches for the pre-selected new words to be learned. This is the only structure of the semantic map that can be pre-determined. The rest of the pattern, association, balance, and emphasis of the words on the map are largely determined by students as apprentice mappers. This in not an artistic challenge to create a beautiful impression with perfect color and harmony, but an organizational challenge to make a spatial structure that accurately represents the conceptual interpretation of the mappers' new knowledge. The conversation of the group largely determines the organizational frame of the map.

After mapping some prior knowledge, read the story or study the picture and think about the new learning the class is taking in. Assimilate this information into the existing structure of the map.

Delegate the process of adding words to the map after the sharing of the read-aloud or picture study. The words generated from the text or picture study become the central ideas of the semantic map or web. At the end of the read-aloud students may associate words in the story to other words they know. Words can be compared and contrasted. Sentences can be rephrased and questions asked about word meanings. Definitions can be given and examples made of correct and incorrect usage of the words.

The students can shake out other supporting words of the text to add to the main collection already on the map. It is important that students help determine some words that may not be central to the story. These are the important words they may encounter in their day-to-day reading/writing across the curriculum.

Once in a while, you might hold back from sharing the list of important words until after the read-aloud or picture study. You might wait until this time to decide on the words for which you can develop a deeper meaning. However, in many occasions you will find it best to hold to implementing the semantic mapping as a two-part process: the scribing of prior knowledge onto the partly prepared semantic map,

Choosing Words for Semantic Mapping

Curriculum Connection: _____

Text or Picture Study: _____

Topic: _____   Text Date: _____

Key words important to understanding the text:

_____

Prior knowledge the students have about this word or its related concepts?

_____

Are the words encountered frequently?

_____

Does the word have multiple meanings (is it polysemous)?

_____

Is the concept significant and does it require pre-teaching?

_____

Can the word be figured out from the context?

_____

Can words be grouped together to enhance the understanding of a concept?

_____

Strategies I employ to help students integrate the word/concept (and related words) into their lives:

_____

Can I make repeated exposures to the word/concept productive and enjoyable?

_____

How can I help students use the word/concept in meaningful ways in multiple contexts?

_____

and the scribing of the information of the read-aloud/picture study. The routine becomes the ritual that comforts and best informs many learners. Despite the routine, engagement and interest remain high because of the careful selection and presentation of a great variety and number of genres and important words.

With the creation of the visual display of important content words, frequently used words, and personal words, we bring together the thoughts and impressions of our entire story-sharing community to create a schema of our understanding. We combine each student's power of thought with that of all the other members of the discourse community to increase everyone's capacity to learn new vocabulary to a deeper conceptual level. The map represents the social and collaborative meanings we have made of the text we have read, the picture we have viewed, or the experience we have shared.

Our students receive high levels of teacher support to create these visual displays of important words. We use explicit teaching to connect and extend the words to support the students' growing level of understanding. They typically benefit from the vigorous, direct, explicit teaching of these semantic maps.

Anchoring the Read-aloud Experience

There are important considerations to make when selecting a read-aloud besides the use of it as a context for the creation of a semantic map for word study. Sometimes read-alouds can be a time for the strategic modeling of an important idea or about what good readers and writers do. Other times, you may want to simply, and only, introduce a book with a brief, relaxed informal conversation. Think carefully whether a semantic map or a pre-reading, during reading, or post reading strategy will work to enrich the read-aloud and contribute to the vocabulary development of students. Sometimes, you will decide to just read it, nothing else. Not every book you read needs to have a semantic map attached to it!

Select read-alouds from a range of fiction, non-fiction, poetry, and biographies that will not only match the interests of your students but also stretch their knowledge, skills, and vocabulary understandings. Choose a variety of lengths of read-alouds, from novels to short stories.

Preparing a Semantic Mapping Strategy

Preparing a Read-aloud Semantic Mapping Strategy

1. Selection
- Select a curriculum-based "big idea" of the essential learning from a Language Arts, Math, Science, or Social Studies curriculum.
- Select a read-aloud with regard to the topic, the genre, the length, the key vocabulary, and taking ample reading and rehearsing time.

2. Word Study
- Select four to six words from the read-aloud suitable to meet the learning needs of the audience. Select other important words.
- Create a large visual display of the semantic map with the topic word and the four to six important words central to it.

3. Visual Literacy (Optional)
- Decide on which pictures you will share along with the read-aloud to support the vocabulary you have selected for study.

Preparing a Picture Study Semantic Mapping Strategy

1. Selection
  - Select a curriculum-based "big idea" of the essential learning from a Language Arts, Math, Science, or Social Studies curriculum.
  - Select a picture with regard to the topic, the genre, the detail, associated key words, and taking ample rehearsing time.

2. Picture Study
  - Select four to six words from the picture study suitable to meet the learning needs of the audience. Select other important words from it as well.
  - Create a large visual display of the semantic map with the topic word and the four to six important words central to it.

3. Other (Optional)
  - Decide on any other pictures, artifacts, or text to share along with the picture to support the key vocabulary you have selected for study.

Method for Semantic Mapping

Method for Read-aloud Semantic Mapping

Use "Checklist for Read-aloud Semantic Mapping Strategy" on page 29.

1. Introduction
  - Sit together with group. Read the book title.
  - Share the semantic mapping of the four to six key words of the read-aloud.
  - Activate prior knowledge of the key words: What do you know about …?
  - Add ideas to the words you have listed on the semantic map.
  - Talk about the genre, word meanings, grammar, and conventions of print of the key words.

2. Before Reading
  - Give the students any other words you think they may be unfamiliar with from the text. Add these to the semantic map.
  - Set a purpose: Listen for these words (read the words on the semantic map).
  - Talk about the genre, word meanings, grammar, and conventions of print of the key words.

3. During Reading
  - Listen to the story.

4. After Reading
  - Ask the students to retell, relate, or reflect on the read-aloud. Use prompts:

I notice…	I know…	I remember…
That reminds me…	I wonder…	What if…

5. Visual Literacy
  - Share some of the interesting pictures and talk about how the

illustrations add to the meaning of the words.

6. *Word Summary*
- Shake out and capture more words on the semantic map.
- Talk about the genre, word meanings, grammar, and conventions of print. Give definitions and examples of correct usage of the key words.

7. *Reader Response*
Share personal connections by telling stories that go with the new vocabulary or storyline.

Method for Picture Study Semantic Mapping

Use "Checklist for Picture Study Semantic Mapping Strategy" on page 30.

1. *Introduction*
- Sit together with group. Share the picture.
- Share the visual display of the four to six key words of the picture study.
- Activate prior knowledge: What do you know about…?
- Add ideas to the words listed on the semantic map.
- Talk about the word meanings, grammar, and conventions of print related to the key words.

2. *Before Studying*
- Give the students any other words you think they may be unfamiliar with from the picture. Add these to the semantic map.
- Set a purpose: Listen for these words (read the words on the semantic map).

3. *During Studying*
- Talk about the picture.

4. *After Studying*
- Ask the students to retell, relate, or reflect on the picture. Use prompts:

  I see…   I notice…   I know…   I remember…
  That reminds me…   I wonder…   What if…

- Talk about the word meanings, grammar, and conventions of print of the key words. Give definitions and examples of correct usage of the key words.

5. *Word Summary*
- Shake out and capture more words on the semantic map.
- Talk about the genre, word meanings, grammar, and conventions of print of these words.

6. *Picture Response*
- Share personal connections by telling stories that go with the vocabulary associated with the picture.

Think very carefully about the audience so that your introduction and read-aloud is situated to flow as a conversation among your particular group of students. Think very carefully about who they are as an audience and what interests they have as individuals.

Checklist for Read-aloud Semantic Mapping Strategy

1. Introduction

❑ Sit together with the group.

❑ Read the book title. Show them the topic on the semantic map.

❑ Point to the 4–6 words. Spell them. Say them out loud.

❑ Ask the students if they know anything about these words.

❑ Map their prior knowledge on the map.

❑ Examine the genre, meaning, grammar, conventions of print of the key words.

2. Before Reading

❑ Identify any other difficult words in the text. Add these to the map.

❑ Set a purpose to listen for the topic words.

3. During Reading

❑ Read the read-aloud.

4. After Reading

❑ Ask the students to retell, relate, or reflect on the key words on the semantic map and add new ideas to it.

| I notice… | I know… | I remember… | That reminds me… |
| I wonder… | What if… | | |

❑ Examine the genre, meaning, grammar, and conventions of print of the key words.

❑ Ask the students to use the key words in a sentence and give examples of correct and incorrect usage.

5. Visual Literacy

❑ Ask the students to identify key words in the picture.

6. Word Summary

❑ Capture more words on the semantic map.

❑ Talk about the genre, word meanings, grammar, and conventions of print. Give definitions and examples of correct usage of the key words.

7. Reader Response

❑ Share personal connections to the words and storyline of the read-aloud.

Checklist for Picture Study Semantic Mapping Strategy

1. Introduction
❑ Sit together with the group.

❑ Show the picture. Show them the topic on the semantic map poster.

❑ Point to the 4–6 key words on the semantic map. Spell them. Say them out loud.

❑ Ask the students if they know anything about these words.

❑ Map their prior knowledge on the map poster.

2. Before Studying
❑ Identify any other associated difficult words in the picture.

❑ Add these to the map.

❑ Set a purpose to listen for the topic words.

3. During Studying
❑ Add more information to the map through discussion of the picture.

4. After Studying
❑ Ask the students to retell, relate, or reflect on the words on the semantic map and add new ideas from the picture study to it.

I see…	I notice…	I know…	I remember…
That reminds me…		I wonder…	What if…

❑ Examine the genre, meaning, grammar, and conventions of print of the key words.

❑ Ask the students to use the key words in a sentence and give examples of correct and incorrect usage.

5. Word Summary
❑ Shake out and capture more words on the semantic map.

❑ Talk about the genre, word meanings, grammar, and conventions of print of these words.

6. Picture Response
❑ Share personal connections by telling stories that go with the vocabulary associated with the picture.

Semantic Mapping Strategies

Students can improve their word knowledge and comprehension through their work with partners or the small groups. Partnerships are especially useful in situations in which a student with an ESL or low socio-economic background can increase their word knowledge and comprehension with peer support.

The mapping strategies presented here can be used with individuals, small groups, or even the entire class. Many of them are designed to have students prepare and share new knowledge of words, phrases, sentences, paragraphs, text, or discourse they have learned with a partner, other groups, or individuals during centres.

You will have to teach the process of mapping to students many times before they can do it independently. Model the step-by-step process during the read-aloud/picture study before having students work with them independently as a centre activity. Some students will need only a few demonstrations to be able to create a map from key words of a story of their choice. Others will need many examples and a carefully selected level of text to be successful. When you first have students create a map, use words they are familiar with. When you feel they are ready, they can apply their mapping to more challenging vocabulary. Eventually they will be able to create semantic maps individually or in small groups working from their own reading material.

Students can use many media to present these semantic mapping strategies. We want them to become routined in the use of the most effective strategies so they can work independently with them during centres. To make things interesting for them, invite them to work with the strategies they have become familiar with and yet challenge them a bit by providing variations in the choice of materials and methods to present them. Students can present their semantic map on a blackboard or whiteboard. They can use an overhead transparency or a computer presentation. They can use various sizes and colors of paper to visually display their new word knowledge.

Using a Dictionary or Thesaurus (page 41)

Create an independent centre to engage students in working with inquiry strategies and a dictionary, visual dictionary, or thesaurus. This strategy is designed to have students support each other in pairs as they learn more about using a dictionary or thesaurus.

Sample Semantic Map from Charlotte's Web

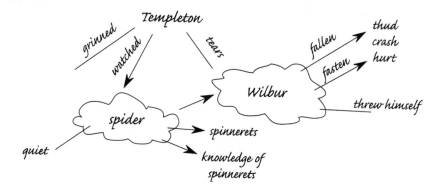

grinned	smiled
watched	looked
spider	arachnid
fasten	tie
fasten	attached?

Prior Knowledge (page 42)

Create a semantic map of what our students already know about the read-aloud topic (adapted from Vacca & Vacca, 1989).

Sample Semantic Map from Charlotte's Web

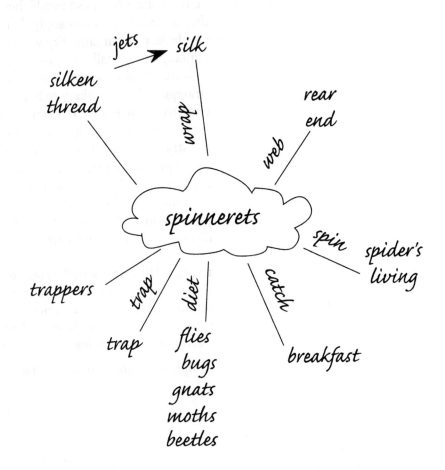

Brainstorming (page 42)

Create a structured semantic map that shares "all" the students' knowledge and experience related to topic, creating interest in the text. Record the words as they are offered.

Sample Semantic Map from Charlotte's Web

Think, Pair, and Share (page 43)

Create a word list designed to have students think about the new words in the text, make personal connections and meanings to the new word, and share the connections and meanings with a partner.

Variation
Partner A can then share what Partner B said with the whole class.
Partner B then shares what Partner A said with the whole class.

Pair and Square Variation
Four partners share what they know about the word and what it reminds them of.

Quotation (page 43)

Create a semantic map of quotations from a story.

Sample Semantic Map from Charlotte's Web

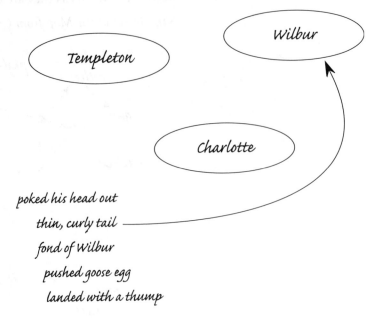

Webbing (page 44)

Create a web from the important words in a story.

Drawing Word Meanings (page 44)

Create this independent word-play centre to engage students in improving their knowledge of words. This strategy is designed to have students support each other in pairs as they draw word meanings together.

Responding Through Drawing (page 45)

Use this independent centre to engage the students in responding to the text through drawing. Reading response is a valuable tool to give a student a voice as a literate person. Students become serious when they are asked to share their opinions. They love to be listened to. This is a perfect opportunity to develop their vocabulary and give them a voice. It respectfully encourages them to share their opinions and feelings.

Mini Word Wall (page 46)

Activities about words in the context of shared reading help children attend to the features of print and the alphabetic nature of English (Ehri, 1992). Create independent centres to engage the students in adding words to the Word Wall that they take from the shared reading text. This strategy is designed to have students support each other in pairs as they take words from the text, categorize them, and add them to the Word Wall.

Sample Mini Word Wall

Frequent Words	Long Words	Tricky Words	Easy Words	New Words
Charlotte	saluta-tions	wrap	spider	Cavatica
Wilbur	near-sighted	trough	legs	blun-dered
the	blun-dered	friendly	all	flashy
I	furiously	eight	me	plunged

Coding the Text (page 47)

Students can use this strategy to become better readers and writers.

Lists of Important Words (page 48)

Create an opportunity for students to use a spelling strategy independently.

Sample List of Important Words

Key Words	
1. grey	grey
2. meet	meet
3. pleased	pleased
4. eagerly	eagerly
5. near	near
6. threads	threads

Working with Word Parts (page 49)

Create an independent centre to engage the students in working with how words represent meaning through combinations of word parts (*run, runner, running*). This strategy is designed to have students support each other in pairs as they learn more word knowledge.

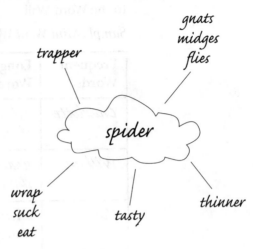

flies	fly	flying	flier
eat	eat	eating	eater
thinner	thin	thinning	
trapper	trap	traps	trapped
early	earlier	earliest	

Vocabulary Anticipation Guide (page 50)

Have students consider their thoughts and opinions of words before they understand the meaning of the word in the context of the read-aloud.

- Create a list of key words for study.
- Insert one key word in each column of the table.
- Write two similar words to the key word in each row.

Sample Vocabulary Anticipation Table from Charlotte's Web

house	(barn) ✓	fair
breeze	(wind) ✓	storm
(rubber boots) ✓	shoes	thongs
sheepfold	stall	(pigpen) ✓
fish	(grain) ✓	hay

Answer Before the Question (page 50)

Create a list of important words from the read-aloud or semantic map on a chart or blackboard.

Sample Answer Before the Question Chart from Charlotte's Web

Answer	Question
"some pig"	What words were spelled?
tremble	What did Mr. Zuckerman begin to do?
pale	How did Edith's face look?
murmured	What sound did Lurvy make?

Word Wall (page 51)

Create a Word Wall from the words you shake out of the text into the semantic map. Talk about and add the words to the Word Wall in specific categories.

Sample Word Wall Categories from Charlotte's Web

High-Frequency Words	Multiple Meaning Words
fair	shaded
Zuckerman	scrambled
his	midway
and	broad

Words with Words in Them	Words with Silent Letters	
Templeton	fr<u>ie</u>nds	i
particularly	pl<u>ea</u>s<u>e</u>d	a, e
Zuckerman	wa<u>t</u>ched	t
Charlotte	pi<u>t</u>ched	t

Same and Different (page 51)

Create a word list designed to have students think about the new words in the text, make personal connections and find meanings for the new word, and share the connections and meanings with a partner.

Sample Semantic Map from Charlotte's Web

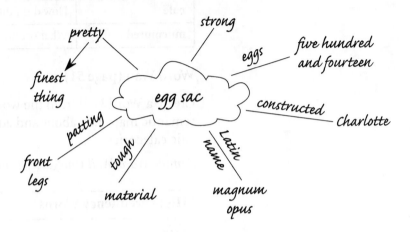

Same	Different
strong, tough	weak
beautiful, pretty	ugly
sac, magnum opus	loose
patted	hit

Webbing Poetry (page 52)

Create a web from the words in a poem.

Sample Poems

The Dreadful Doings of Jelly Belly

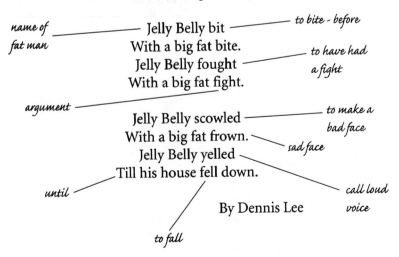

Venn Diagram (page 52)

Create a Venn diagram comparing and contrasting a concept from the read-aloud.

Sample from Charlotte's Web

Wilbur		Charlotte
Different	**Same**	**Different**
	need to eat	
grown big	Wilbur	remains small
baby	Wilbur	adult
	friendly	

Structured Overview (page 53)

Create an overview by brainstorming words and then categorizing them.

Sample from Charlotte's Web
Important Topic Word(s): Animal Characters in *Charlotte's Web*

Brainstormed Words: Wilbur, flies, geese, ducks, cow, rat, butterflies, Charlotte, chickens, horses, donkeys, moths, spiders, pigs, sows, crickets, fish, sheep, goslings, gander, potato bug, beetles, gnats, midges, mosquitoes, crickets, lamb, Templeton

↕

Live in house	Live in _____	Live in barn	Live in pasture	Live in barnyard
Wilbur		geese		ducks
		cow		chicken
		horses		
		flies		

Story Starter (page 54)

Create a display of words to go with each part of the story.

Story Frame (page 55)

Create a story frame that shows the important key words from the read-aloud.

Know–Wonder–Learn (page 56)

Create active roles before, during, and after the read-aloud for your students to frame their thinking as they learn to ask questions and assess their own learning.

Window Pane (page 57)

Create a window pane to show some of the multi-leveled words in the read aloud.

Story Pyramid (page 57)

Create a pyramid of important key words from the story.

Sample from Charlotte's Web

Wilbur
"some pig"
wants to live
web to safe life
best pig at the fair
Charlotte leaves a sac of eggs

Semantic Mapping: Using a Dictionary or Thesaurus

Strategy: Good spellers use a dictionary, visual dictionary, or thesaurus.

1. Work in partners to find other easier and harder versions of key words in a dictionary or a thesaurus.

2. See it: Write a semantic map word for your partner.

3. Say it: Say it together slowly with your partner.

4. Write it: Both partners look and see if they can find another version of the word.

5. Box the tricky parts, the important parts, or unusual parts of each word.

6. Close your eyes.

7. Visualize the word in your mind.

Repeat for each of the words you are sharing.

Key Words	
1.	
2.	
3.	
4.	
5.	
6.	

Semantic Mapping: Prior Knowledge

Strategy: Good readers think about what they know about a topic before they read.

1. List important key words on the chart.
2. Everyone calls out what they already know about the word.
3. At the end of the read-aloud, review the brainstorm to see if there is any new information not listed in the original one.

Semantic Mapping: Brainstorming

Strategy: Good readers try out all the ideas they think of.

1. Look at the key words.
2. Everyone calls out what they already know about the word.
3. At the end of the read-aloud, students review the brainstorm to see if there is any new information to be listed.

Semantic Mapping: Think, Pair, and Share

Strategy: Good readers think about the important words in a story.

1. Take a blank sheet of paper and fold it into four boxes.
2. Sit in partners and select an important word from the semantic map.
3. Draw pictures of the multiple meanings of these words.
4. Talk together about what meaning each picture shows.

Semantic Mapping: Quotation

Strategy: Good readers have lots of ideas on what they read.

1. Pick your quotations from the text.
2. List them on the map for your partner.
3. Write in the characters from the text.
4. Talk quietly about your ideas.
5. Decide what quotes go with each character.
6. Make a line from the quotation to the character.

Semantic Mapping: Webbing

Strategy: Good readers have lots of ideas.

1. Sit in partners. Read a page of a text.
2. Select a topic and add four to six key words to represent the branches of the semantic map.
3. Trade page of text and semantic maps.
4. Read the story you receive.
5. Draw a semantic map with the key words your partner gave you.
6. Trade back papers and view each other's semantic map.

Semantic Mapping: Drawing Word Meanings

Strategy: Good readers use pictures to help them understand.

1. Take a blank sheet of paper and fold it into four boxes.
2. Sit in partners and select an important word from the semantic map.
3. Draw pictures of the multiple meanings of these words.
4. Talk together about what meaning each picture shows.

Semantic Mapping: Responding Through Drawing

Strategy: Good readers respond to the words they read.

1. Sit in partners and select an idea from the following prompts:
   - something personal
   - something you liked
   - something you found interesting
   - the place or setting
   - a person or character
   - a word you can touch
   - a word you cannot touch
   - something important to you
   - something you now know that you didn't before

2. Take a blank sheet of paper and fold it into four boxes.
3. Draw pictures of the things you chose. Label them.
4. Talk together about what you have drawn.

Semantic Mapping: Mini Word Wall

Strategy: Good readers know how to categorize words.
Good readers know about words.

1. Sit in partners with your shared reading text.
2. Pick a prompt from a STRETCH chart.
3. Think and search through the text for responses to the prompt. Repeat for additional prompts.
4. Add these words to the Mini Word Wall.
5. Check carefully that the spelling is right.

Frequent Words	Long Words	Tricky Words	Easy Words	New Words

Semantic Mapping: Coding the Text

Strategy: Good readers think and search through the text they read to understand it.

1. Partner up.

2. Decide together on a STRETCH chart.

3. Select a prompt from the chart.

4. Respond to the prompt in one of the following ways::
   - **Right There** on the page
   - **Think and Search** using clues on the page and your own thoughts
   - **On My Own** relating to the page from your own experience

4. Have your partner share his or her ideas related to the prompt.

5. Both partners highlight selected conventions, words, or sentences.

6. Talk briefly about what you understand about today's text.

Semantic Mapping: Lists of Important Words

Strategy: Good spellers get to know words by looking at them, saying them, and writing them.

1. Partner up.

2. See it: Write a key word in the first column.

3. Say it: Say it together slowly with your partner.

4. Write it: Both partners look at it and write it down in the second column.

5. Box the tricky parts, the important parts, or unusual parts of each word.

6. Close your eyes. Visualize the word in your mind.

Repeat for each of the words you are sharing.

Key Words	
1.	
2.	
3.	
4.	
5.	
6.	

Semantic Mapping: Working with Word Parts

Strategy: Good spellers know about combinations of words.

1. Work in partners to create as many combinations for words as you can.

2. See it: Write a semantic map word in the first column.

3. Say it: Say it together slowly with your partner.

4. Write it: Write combination words it in the second column.

5. Box the tricky parts, the important parts, or unusual parts of each word.

6. Underline the new word parts.

7. Close your eyes. Visualize the word in your mind.

Repeat for each of the words you are sharing.

Key Words	
1.	
2.	
3.	
4.	
5.	
6.	

Semantic Mapping: Vocabulary Anticipation Guide

Strategy: Good readers anticipate what is going to happen.

1. Look at the table of words. Choose and circle one word out of each three that you think best fits the meaning of the word.

2. After the story or picture study, go back to the table and put a check mark beside the word you now think best fits the read-aloud.

3. Check against your original choices and see if what you picked then is still best, or if your opinion of the word meaning has changed.

Semantic Mapping: Answer Before the Question

Strategy: Good readers have questions about a story.

1. One partner will call out a key word from the text.

2. The other partner will come up with questions that fit the answer that has been given.

Answer	Question

Semantic Mapping: Word Wall

Strategy: Good readers think about types of words.

1. Find words in the text to answer the prompts on the STRETCH charts. Highlight them.
2. Decide where on the Word Wall each word should be listed.
3. List the words on the Word Wall.
4. Remind each other to use the Word Wall independently as a tool for your own writing.

Semantic Mapping: Same and Different

Strategy: Good readers play with ideas.

1. Have your partner read the key words on the semantic map.
2. Think: What is the same?
3. Think: What is different?
4. Write your ideas on each list.
5. Share your ideas.

Same	Different

Semantic Mapping: Webbing Poetry

Strategy: Good readers work hard to understand the dense language of poetry.

1. Pick your poem. Underline the key words to be mapped.
2. Trade poems with a partner.
3. Make lines and arrows to the underlined words in the poem.
4. Give meanings to these words in the margin.
5. Talk quietly about your ideas to your partner.
6. Decide on the other ideas it reminds you of.

Semantic Mapping: Venn Diagram

Strategy: Good readers have lots of good ideas to compare and contrast.

1. Take turns listing your ideas.
2. Tell each other your ideas.
3. Read each other's ideas.
4. Talk quietly about your ideas.

_____   _____

Different	Same	Different

Semantic Mapping: Structured Overview

Strategy: Good readers have lots of good ideas they need to sort.

1. Make a list of brainstormed words with your partner.
2. Decide on categories, or use categories provided. Place each word in a category.
3. Share each other's ideas on why you have placed them there.
4. Talk quietly about your ideas.

Important Topic Word: _____

Brainstormed Words:

_____

_____

_____

Categories:

Semantic Mapping: Story Starter

Strategy: Good readers have lots of good ideas.

1. Take turns listing your ideas about the story.

2. Tell each other your ideas.

3. Write down your ideas.

4. Talk quietly about your ideas.

The problem is	The first thing that happened...	The next thing that happened...	The story ends when...	The exciting part is when...

Semantic Mapping: Story Frame

Strategy: Good readers think about the parts of the story.

1. Fold a paper into four boxes.
2. Draw and label the characters.
3. Draw and label the setting.
4. Draw and label the problem.
5. Draw and label the ending.
6. Share your ideas.

Characters	Setting
Problem	**Ending**

Semantic Mapping: Know-Wonder-Learn

Strategy: Good readers think about what they know and ask questions.

1. Write what you know.
2. Ask questions about things you wonder about: What do you want to find out?
3. Write what you learned.
4. Write what you still want to know.

I know...	I wonder...	I learned...

I know...	I wonder...	I learned...

Semantic Mapping: Window Pane

Strategy: Good readers make pictures in their mind.

1. Take a sheet of paper and fold it into four.
2. Look at the semantic map. Select an important key word.
3. Think of the pictures you have in your mind.
4. Draw these pictures in the "window pane" squares on the paper. Label them.
5. Share part of the story and your picture with the class.

Semantic Mapping: Story Pyramid

Strategy: Good readers can summarize the story.

1. Think about the story.
2. Name the character (one word).
3. Describe the character (two words).
4. Describe the problem (three words).
5. Describe the main event (four words).
6. Describe another event (five words).
7. Describe how the story is resolve (six words).
8. Reread your Story Pyramid.

Chapter 4: STRETCH-Chart Prompted Conversations

We model interest and enthusiasm for word knowledge and analysis, and show the importance of extensive reading, through shared reading. We use STRETCH charts to prompt conversation during shared reading as the second important strategy of a consistent, explicit, and extensive system of vocabulary instruction to make words stick. Coding and highlighting the text we talk about using STRETCH charts may seem like a simple strategy, but the depth and level of conversation we can generate with our students can anchor much of the word knowledge we want our students to acquire.

Shared reading comes between the reading "to" the students during semantic mapping and the reading "by" of independent word play. In the first strategy, the read-aloud, students have little responsibility to make decisions about the text; in the last, the independent centres, students have full responsibility to read every word accurately and independently. In shared reading, we read and converse "with" students to analyze word meaning in texts. Instructional contexts like this get students started on their own reading, writing, and serious word play. For students who are linguistically disadvantaged, this daily ritual, for the extensive analyzing of text "with" them, gives them many rich opportunities to deepen and enrich their own word knowledge.

Grand Conversations

Biemiller (2002a) indicates that teachers of young children spend relatively little time thoroughly analyzing word meaning in texts. Teachers are reported to address unknown words mainly through context-based "mentioning," a process of simply providing a context-specific definition and short-lived conversation with the students about the word in similar contexts. These pithy conversations rarely lead to more in-depth analysis of the words or the exploration of other contexts words may be used in.

In our word-anchoring program we spend time each day thoroughly analyzing word meanings in texts, engaging students in "grand conversations" (Eeds & Wells, 1989) during prompted shared reading. We extend the definitions of words during conversations that may last anywhere from fifteen minutes with primary students to an hour with intermediates. This is the time students analyze word meanings in the shared reading text and talk about it in ways that further their thinking about the words.

According to best-practice research, participation in a discourse community is crucial for the cultivation of deeper levels of vocabulary knowledge. Fu and Townsend (1999) remind us that our students' language learning is "fuelled by their curiosity and their desire to connect and communicate with others." Eeds and Wells (1989) define grand conversations as those that occur when we allow our students to share multiple interpretations of the text. They give a deeper and more enriched understanding the text than the "inquisition model, which assumes that a correct interpretation exists that is known to the teacher and is to be discovered by the students" (Eeds & Wells, 1989).

Talk about text is a great alternative to work sheets. It is not enough to read a text and respond to it in written form. Our students need to construct more meaning of what they read and develop a personal significance to it. As students share their personal comments, other students are prompted to share their experiences, interpretations, and ideas. As a result, they are socially constructing the meaning of what they have read. With the conversations of shared reading, students are typically able to

- see the relationship between the text and content (pragmatics)
- see the relationship between the ideas and the words (semantics)
- use each other as a resource to clarify word meanings (semantics)
- see the relationship between words, including organizational features, such as phrasing, sentence structure, use of linking words, paragraphs, discourse (syntax)
- represent ideas on the page, make sense of print (graphophonics)
- gain knowledge of graphic symbols to represent ideas on the page (graphophonics)
- see letter–sound relationships (graphophonics)
- see spelling patterns (graphophonics)
- understand directionality of print (graphophonics)
- understand spacing and text layout (graphophonics)
- find significance in the text
- find purpose in the text
- have fun with the text
- hear others' opinions; share multiple interpretations to extend their own thinking
- become better readers and writers
- remember what is read; have the words stick

Scaffolding the Conversations

Implementing these grand conversations into your teaching practice can be challenging. Students traditionally have limited opportunity to talk in school. In many cases, the teacher does most of the talking. When students do talk, they do not typically have the language to participate in conversations at deep levels.

The first conversations you have about the text will likely not be rich and thoughtful without some careful scaffolding. Just as students need

Shared reading can be a generatic context in which students talk about their responses in ways they would not otherwise reveal.

It may take you several weeks to a month to explain, model, and guide the practices of the discourse community before they go smoothly on their own.

59

to be trained to be semantic mappers, they also need to be trained to participate in the discourse community. Students profit from lots of modeling by the teacher to learn how to converse effectively. Modeling how to respond to some of the prompts during read-alouds and your first shared reading events may not be enough to get them talking about the huge range of possibilities for "knowing a word." You will need to scaffold the students' practice with talk about text until they become more comfortable and knowledgeable about words and about the process of sharing this knowledge. Organizing complex learning environments such as this may take lots of careful planning, but eventually, when you see how empowered your students are, you will consider it worth it. It takes time and effort but it can be done!

The Shared Reading Routine

The first part of the Shared Reading routine is for the teacher to take a few minutes to introduce the author, title, and genre. Marie Clay (1993) suggests that "the introduction should be viewed as a time when the teacher prepares the reader to enter into a conversation with the author of the text." Enter this conversation by walking the students through the text, looking briefly at the title and the passage, and discussing any special aspects of it. Give a brief summary of the text in two or three statements to once again activate the students' background knowledge and set them into a semantic or meaning-based cueing system. Establish the purpose for reading the text with the audience — what's in it for them — and establish how it will read it. Briefly implant a text outline and draw attention to important, difficult, unique vocabulary or any points of interest before beginning the formal reading and talking about the text.

Narrow the amount of text to one page, to control the amount of information that is being covered.

Guided/Prompted Conversations

One relatively simple, effective means to scaffold our students' movement towards grand conversations is accomplished by providing prompts to facilitate their talk about text. Much as the semantic map serves as a graphic organizer of a read-aloud/picture study, STRETCH charts, poster-size sets of prompts for conversation, serve as a discourse organizer for the shared reading community. The Primary and Intermediate charts in Chapter 5 are designed to engage students in the active analysis of the shared reading words, calling attention to their component letters, sounds, shapes, and meaning, and the background knowledge students may have about them. The prompts focus the students' attention on the multiplicity of word meanings and secure a deeper level of word knowledge than single-meaning instructional approaches.

STRETCH charts and associated conversations are designed to s-t-r-e-t-c-h or expand students' deeper reflection and conceptualization of word knowledge. We want to cultivate reflection and the way that we do this is by immersing students in talk — talk about their experiences, talk about their ideas, talk about words — for it is through talk that we develop the ability to reflect. We wrap talk in, through, and around experiences to help them develop the ability to reflect in action, and we talk afterwards (debrief) to develop the ability to reflect on action (Chapman, 1997).

Using STRETCH charts, students can explore almost all of the subsystems of written language:

- Pragmatics: registers, functions, and forms of representations, genres
- Semantics: the meaning vocabulary; the relationship between ideas, words, and their meaning
- Syntax: the way words are organized, phrasing, sentence structure, paragraphs, grammar
- Graphophonics: representation of ideas on the page, conventions of print, spelling patterns, letter sound–shape relationship, directionality

Students are motivated to practise word study skills contextually with student-centred prompted conversations. Exploring the dimensions of written language holistically can be an interesting and informative literacy experience for students. Many are highly engaged in exploring all these dimensions of written language when they are placed at the enter of the interesting conversations — when they are doing most of the talking, not the teacher. They find it challenging to find the words to share new knowledge about their discoveries coming to know words. This is a situated, social, and active method for them to explore the text.

Guidelines for Prompted Conversations

- Stories/conversation need to be meet with acceptance and respect.
- Allow the transaction between the teacher, student, and story by allowing students to explore and trust their own responses, thoughts, and feeling.
- Encourage students to explore their stories in terms of public and private concerns, questions, and opinions.
- Use these stories as a learning context for students who are new to English.
- Include everyone in a sitting arrangement that creates a comfortable sense of belonging.
- Allow at-risk, low-progress students to preview the shared reading text before the prompted conversations.
- Allow the talk-alouds of the story sharing to flow; some may run longer that others.
- Allow time for students to respond to the stories they head.
- Connect the stories so they have a repertoire of stories over the year.
- Adapt the STRETCH charts (in Chapter 5) to meet the vocabulary learning needs of the particular group of students.

Arrange for the shared reading program to be predictable in the time, routine, materials, and setting so that it can include members of the school-based learning assistance team to support at-risk, learning disabled, ESL and low-progress students in their regular classrooms.

Routine for STRETCH-chart Prompted Conversation

See "Checklist for STRETCH-chart Prompted Conversation" on page 64.

Time for prompted conversations invites students to have a strong voice in anchoring key words themselves.

1. *Introduction*

   Give everyone individual copies of the shared reading text.

2. *Shared Reading*
   - Introduce the shared reading text: author, title, and genre.
   - Look briefly through the title and text.
   - Give a brief summary of the text (brief).
   - Point to important, different, unique vocabulary.
   - Note any points of interest; e.g., special conventions of print.

3. *Prereading*
   - Review semantic map of key words from the read-aloud or picture study. Set a purpose for the class to read the shared reading text.

4. *Reading*
   - Read the shared text with the class.
   - During Reading Strategies: review reading strategies good readers use.

5. *After Reading*
   - Use the STRETCH chart to guide the students' talk about the text.

6. *Discussion*
   - Highlight (code) various aspects of the text.
   - Highlight (code) vocabulary.
   - Encourage lots of sharing of students' responses to the prompts (See Routine for Coding the Text, page 69).

Context: *Shared Reading*
Shared Reading Text: *Excerpt from* Scarecrow
Important Concept Words: wonder, witness, real, mammoth, borrowed
Strategy: *Conversations/Discussions Prompted by STRETCH Charts*
Level of Instruction: *Teacher-directed or student-directed, shared responsibility for learning*
Grouping: *Whole group/ small group*

I strategically select an excerpt from the *Scarecrow* read-aloud/picture study as our shared reading text, so that I can effectively take the second pass at exposing my students to important vocabulary. I carefully prepare a 8.5" x 11" page excerpt from Cynthia Rylant's text. All the important new words we are learning are in the text, along with a range of high-interest words and common everyday words suitable for my linguistically disadvantaged students. The print is spaced with lots of room for the students to highlight/code the words, phrases, sentences, and conventions of print. I have left lots of margin room so they can draw symbols and pictures to assist their meaning-making during the 45-minute shared reading event. Finally, I add a list of key words at the bottom of the page.

He knows he isn't real. A scarecrow understands right away that he is just borrowed parts made to look like somebody.

But he knows this, too: that there is a certain wonder going on around him. Seeds are being planted, and inside them there are ten-foot-tall sunflowers and mammoth pumpkins and beans that just go on forever.

And though the scarecrow knows that he can as quickly be turned back into straw and buttons as he was turned into a man, he doesn't care.

He has been with the owls in evening and the rabbits at dawn. He has watched the spider at work for hours making a web like lace. He has seen the sun tremble and the moon lie still.

The scarecrow doesn't care what he is made of or how long he might last, for he has been a witness to life. The earth has rained and snowed and blossomed and wilted and yellowed and greened and vined itself all around him. His hat has housed mice and his arms have rested birds. A morning glory has held tight to his legs and a worm is living in his lapel.

There is not much else a person might want, and the scarecrow knows this.

Borrowed wonder witness mammoth real

The students use brightly colored highlighters and colored felt pens to code the text as we talk about it. They consult a STRETCH chart of conversation prompts to assist them with their talk about text. A copy of the text is also on the overhead projector so that all the students can check their place as we explore various aspects of it.

The students sit in groups of four, as shoulder partners, to support each other as they collaborate to talk about the *Scarecrow* text. Adam stands ready to add the words we code to the Word Wall. I stand ready to support Angela who, as student-as-teacher, willingly moderates over the talk about the text with the help of the STRETCH charts. She has the security of knowing she can refer to this list of conversation prompts or ask me to help her "work" the meaning making of the text

The goal of the shared reading conversation, like that of the read-aloud, is to have the students increase their general word knowl-edge and recognition, and to improve their ability to discriminate the nuances in the meanings of words. We code the *Scarecrow* excerpt to bring important learning of the letter shapes, sounds, and word parts to the close attention of all the students. Whole-class shared reading — talking about the text, coding the text, and classifying the text — is an engaging way to make meaning of the big ideas of "witnessing" and "wondering", and perhaps, of ourselves, each other, and the world.

Highlighting/Coding the Text

I ask the students to find a word with a long shape. Angela decides that *scarecrow* is the longest word with nine letters. Adam jumps in that *sunflowers* is ten letters and *blossomed* is nine. Angela asks if *scarecrow* counts as a long word because it is two words put together. We decide that a compound word is a long word and go on to look for some other compound words. The students are amazed at how many compound words there are on this page.

I ask the students to find words that start with a *w*. They find the words *witness, wonder, worm, want, watched*, and *wilted* on their individual pages, and highlight all of these. I ask the students what is the same about them and what is different. Jamie decides that some of the words have a suffix of *-ed*. We now think and search through the text for other words that have similar endings. We find lots of words with the *-ed* suffix: *borrowed, turned, rained, snowed, blossomed, wilted, yellowed, greened, vined, housed*, and *rested*. I want the students to think about the shapes and sounds and meaning of many of the words, and compare and contrast them to other words. With some prompts, they are required to highlight a number of bits throughout the text.

The students decide to draw a little icon of a bed above each of the words with an *-ed* ending. Adam loves to actually make the little picture. He will use this little picture as a memory hook when writing a word where he hears the "d" sound at the end of the word. If he can think of the bed tool, he may remember to print the *-ed* instead of *-d*.

The students are highly engaged in their Think and Search challenges, and are more confident talking about their word knowledge each day we have shared reading. They seem content to take turns and listen to one another as they think and search for words. One of the things I notice is that, in Adam's efforts to make his understandings about words meaningful to others, he reaches a fuller understanding of the dimensions of the words himself.

Angela also guides the revisiting of the words from the semantic map we created from the read-aloud/picture study to anchor further development of important word concepts. If the students have only partial word knowledge, I can choose to spend more time prompting them to increase their understanding.

We use conversations to explore the sound, structure, and multiple meanings of the not only the key words of *witness, wonder, mammoth, borrowed*, and *real*, but the frequently used, personal choice words of individuals in the class. Working at highlighting/coding the letters with different sounds, structures, and meanings helps the students understand how words work and remember them. It is engaging for them to become detectives, thinking about the prompts and searching for evidence in the text to support their learning of their special, important words.

Checklist for STRETCH-chart Prompted Conversation

Introduction

❑ Make sure everyone has a copy of the shared reading text.

Shared Reading

❑ Introduce the shared reading text. Walk through the text.

❑ Introduce the shared reading text: author, title and genre.

❑ Look briefly through the title and text.

❑ Give brief summary of the text (brief).

❑ Point to important, different, unique vocabulary.

❑ Note any points of interest; e.g., special conventions of print.

Prereading

❑ Set a purpose for the class to read the shared reading text.

Reading

❑ Choral read the text with the whole class.

Or

❑ Listen as groups of students read the text to the rest of the class.

❑ Talk about your attempts to problem solve words, figure out words, and use reading behaviors and strategies of good readers (review reading strategies good readers use).

Using STRETCH Charts

❑ Select a STRETCH Chart.

❑ Ask students to look at the STRETCH Chart.

❑ Select a prompt.

❑ Ask students to think about a response to the prompt.

❑ Give "wait time."

❑ Have students highlight their responses on their hard copy of the shared reading text.

Coding/Highlighting the Text

❑ Have students use codes and highlighting to make special meaning of some of the text.

Word Wall

❑ Add some of the words shared in the discussion to the Word Wall

Knowledge of a word includes knowing how it sounds, how it is written, and how it is used in parts of speech. It also means the exposure to its polysemy — or multiple meanings — and its morphology — or derivations. Only in this way do students fully acquire the word as part of their vocabulary (Nagy & Scott, 2000; Nation, 1990). The list reviews the kind of word knowledge the students acquire with the STRETCH charts.

Sample of STRETCH-chart Prompted Word Knowledge

- Circle a word that is long/two-word (structure): scarecrow, understands
- Box a word with a tall shape (structure): still and all
- Circle a word that starts with the letter w (phonics): wonder, with, web, witness
- Box a word you can sound out (phonics): his, has, sun, is, just, can, as, him
- Box a word you cannot sound out (phonics): right, might, tight (gh); watched (t)
- Box a word you didn't know before (meaning): glory, vined, witness, excerpt
- Underline a person (grammar): person, him, Rylant, somebody, man
- Underline a place (grammar): web, sun, moon, lapel, hat
- Underline a thing (grammar): beans, pumpkin, button, spider, scarecrow
- Box a hard word (grammar): tight, certain, knows, mammoth
- Circle an easy/everyday/common word (word meaning): man, care, legs, and
- Box a word you had to jump over/come back to (strategies): excerpt
- Star a word that has a tricky spelling (strategies): dawn, tight
- Star a word you like (meaning): spider, scarecrow, witness, pumpkin
- Cross out a word you don't like (meaning): spider, beans
- Circle a 3-syllable word (structure): un-der-stands, e-ven-ing
- Box a word with a suffix (structure): vined, wilted, blossomed, yellowed
- Slice through a compound word (structure): scare/crow, under/stands, a/round

Shared Responsibility

Shared reading is a less robust kind of teaching, as the students share a lot of responsibility to talk about the shared text. I expect a moderate to high level of understanding for the students participating in this shared reading event because the work we do in exploring the text is done so thoroughly. The engagement increases somewhat from the read-aloud with the more student-centred activity.

Even very young students can be taught to lead the talk about the text. With STRETCH charts in the hands of the students, they can efficiently and effectively lead their own discussions about the shared reading text, and take on a role of shared responsibility for the prompted conversations about word knowledge.

There are numerous leadership roles for the students during the shared reading event. The teacher's role initially may be to review the expectations of the behavior of the students during shared reading and teaching all the components of it. Over time you may wish to withdraw into a supporting role, with the students taking over the talk about the text. You can enlist a student into the role of teacher to take responsibility for the leading of the shared reading event. The students can moderate over the shared reading, select the appropriate STRETCH chart for the conversation, lead the coding of the text, and tally new words on the Word Wall. It will take time to transfer responsibility over to them for the independent management of the shared reading event. You will develop more vocabulary of more students if you turn over the leading of the shared reading event to a student-as-teacher. If you can withdraw from the leadership role and have students take turns moderating the talk about text, they will learn more about words than they could ever learn from listening to you.

The STRETCH charts are invaluable for scaffolding the students in their new role of shared responsibility for high engagement with the text. This scaffolding helps the student-as-teacher maintain the quality of the conversation as we shift to the role of leading from behind. The STRETCH charts are efficient and effective in assisting our students so they can slip comfortably into their new leadership role. They can support either teacher or students as leader of the prompted shared reading until they are able to effectively lead the conversation, code the text, and add new vocabulary to the Word Wall.

When you decide to entirely relinquish your role and responsibility for the discussion of word knowledge, and it is largely in the hands of the students, you will have the luxury of time to support one child or a group of students who may struggle to attend to understanding this new knowledge. You can also choose to sit entirely outside the group, using this kid-watching time to inform your teaching. Once in a while, you may suddenly decide to be included, taking a brief active role for a "teachable moment" to introduce new thoughts and feelings, clear up misconceptions, and nurture a deeper understanding of a particular word, phrase, or sentence. Without the STRETCH charts, you remain in an active teaching role with full responsibility for the prompted conversations and having the students assume a passive role.

With the support of the STRETCH charts, the talk becomes learner-centred and yet the students are still able to focus the conversation at a meaningful level. With the support of the appropriate level of prompts, this guided participation in talk about text can be used with students in Grades from 1 to 8. The students typically are challenged to "lead to learn," to become more skilled at communicating and sharing their word knowledge.

Chapter 5: Using STRETCH Charts

The reference set for prompted conversations at the end of this chapter consists of 30 STRETCH charts of prompts that serve to organize discourse in communities from Grade 1 to Grade 8. The set is broken into two collections, one for Primary students Grades 1–3 (pages 75–85) and the other for Intermediate students Grades 4–8 (pages 76–102). However, these are only guidelines, and it is up to you, as the teacher, to decide which STRETCH charts are most suitable for use with a particular grade and level of students. It may be necessary to select prompts from a variety and number of charts to make a personalized STRETCH chart to meet the needs of a particular group of students. A form is provided (page 103) for teachers to use in customizing a Composite STRETCH Chart for use with a particular class. Composite STRETCH charts add some variety to the shared reading event.

The charts can be enlarged and posted on the wall in easy view of all the participants in the shared reading. They can be copied and laminated into a set for selection by the students-as-teachers. They can be placed on the overhead or used on a projector.

Time for Prompted Conversations
Kindergarten to Early Primary:
   15–20 minutes
Late Primary 30–45 minutes
Intermediate 45–60 minutes

The shared reading may vary in length according to the depth and breadth of conversation that arises. For most early primary classes, the students' conversations can be sustained for 15–20 minutes. Late primary students participate as a discourse community for slightly longer periods of time, increasing their time spent to 30–45 minutes. Intermediate classes can maintain their engagement for up to an hour.

Getting Started

Give each student their own copy of the text on which to highlight the vocabulary you shake out of your guided discussions. They will highlight the text, or code it with symbols, as you discuss it. As they mark the page with a highlighter, they participate in student-centred conversations that stretch their new word knowledge and allow them to talk aloud about the strategies they use to read the words, phrases, and sentences. As students code the text with symbols — ones that, ideally, they have invented together with the teacher — they are actively involved in broadening their overall comprehension of the story. The students get to touch the language as well as see it, hear it, and speak about it. The colors help them notice important information and points about the conventions of the print.

Coding the Text

In September, collaborate as a class to devise a key for coding the text to be used throughout the year. You may decide to use circles to code evidence of genre in the text (pragmatics). You may decide to use small icons drawn above the words being discussed, such as the image of a letter above a word in the text with an "er" in it (graphophonics). This new "er" word can be added to the "er" Word Family column on the Word Wall (graphophonics). Students can use a plus (+) over words they know the meaning of, and a minus (-) over words that they do not know (semantics). Students can use several colors of highlighters to mark the grammar (syntax) on the shared reading text. They can box examples of conventions of print such as punctuation, capital letters, and italicized words (graphophonics). These are only a few ideas for ways students can code the shared reading text.

Students appreciate being able to design the coding system to use on the shared reading text.

Strategies for Retrieving Information

Students have several options of strategies they use to respond to the conversation prompts and code the text. The Right There strategy is the most straightforward method for our students to retrieve information. With this strategy, they locate the information they are looking for "right there" in the text and highlight it. This prompt calls for the students to highlight a single word or phrase in the text, and the conversation revolves around it.

The Think and Search strategy is a little more complicated. With this one, the students search through the text and highlight/code different bits of information to respond to the prompt. Sometimes their response also goes beyond what can be viewed or marked on the text. This is an inferential process, by which they make sense of the text beyond what is on the page. This prompts students to highlight several parts of the text and use more conversation to discuss how they are connected.

The third strategy, the On My Own Strategy, requires a higher level of thinking. Students formulate a response that may be prompted from a single word they highlight on the text, but the response comes largely from their own reflection. This strategy largely relates to the students' own experience. Most of the information cannot be found and highlighted in the shared reading text. This prompt, although it involves little coding of the text, often leads to higher-level thinking and more in-depth conversation. Each different STRETCH prompt gives a student practice with the metacognition — the thinking about their thinking of how good readers retrieve information.

Strategies to Retrieve Information
***Right There* Coding:** *little coding, limited response*
***Think and Search* Coding:** *coding throughout different parts of the text, increased response*
***On My Own* Coding:** *little coding with longer, deeper response*

Routine for Coding Text

Many of the words we shake out of our prompted conversations can be added to the Word Wall as they are coded. This is one more important step in vocabulary instruction. The Word Wall, along with the semantic mapping the students have done, becomes another part of the growing visual display of word knowledge for the students.

Use "Checklist for Coding Text" on page 70.

1. Select a STRETCH Chart
- Ask students to look at the STRETCH Chart

2. Select a Prompt
- Ask students to think about a response to the selected prompt.

3. Highlight Text
- Give "wait time."
- Have students highlight their responses on their hard copy of the shared reading text.

4. Select a Student Response
- Ask students to stand and share their responses with the class.

5. All Students Highlight Text
- Ask all students to highlight/code the word, phrase, etc.

6. Use the Overhead
- Have one student at the overhead model the highlighting of the part of the text being discussed.

7. Add Word to the Word Wall
- Have all the students watch as the word is added to the Word Wall.

6. Select Other Students
- Ask other students to share their responses with the class. Highlight these.

7. Select a New Prompt
- Ask the students to respond to the next prompt, and repeat the process.

STRETCH-Chart Strategies

The reference set of STRETCH charts consists of more than 20 strategies to focus the attention of the readers to the text. It is up to you as the teacher to decide on the strategy that will best serve the needs of your students to develop their roles as literate persons.

Having students actively engaged with a highlighter to code the text of the prompted conversation is one way to keep everyone actively engaged in their meaning-making.

Aesthetic Strategies

- Talking About Feelings and Attitudes, page 75
- Interpreting Images, Feelings, and Attitudes of the Text, pages 86, 87

Use these STRETCH charts to extend students' fascination with the feeling of the words, to enjoy working with the words, to ponder the words and what they mean to them, to make personal connections to

Checklist for Method to Code the Text

❑ Select a STRETCH chart.

❑ Ask students to look at the selected STRETCH chart.

❑ Select a prompt.

❑ Ask students to think about a response to this prompt

❑ Give "wait time."

❑ Have students highlight their responses on their hard copy of the shared reading text.

❑ Select a student response.

❑ Ask the student to stand and share their response with the class.

❑ Draw attention to the overhead.

❑ Have one student at the overhead model the highlighting of the part of the text being discussed.

❑ Add the word to the Word Wall.

❑ Ask students to watch as the word is added to the Word Wall.

❑ Ask other students to share their responses with the class. Highlight these.

❑ Select a new prompt and repeat the process with other prompts.

them. These STRETCH charts extend students' understanding of the special personal rewards of print. Talking about personal connections teaches students how good readers assume the important role of text participant.

Metacognitive Strategies

- Talking About Our Thinking, page 76
- Interpreting Our Thinking Strategies, page 88

Use these STRETCH charts to engage students in talk-alouds about self-monitoring operations of self-correction and confirmation of the words they are reading. They need to use several skills in combination to read, since no single skill is typically reliable. They can discuss their predictive operations (their ability to use context to fill the slots of unknown words) and structural operations to follow the plot, causal sequences, and logical arrangements. Talking about the metacognition of systematic cross-checking of skills teaches students how good readers think about their thinking as they read, and helps them assume the important role of text participant.

Phonological Strategies

Enclosing a letter within oblique lines indicates that it is the sound being discussed, not the letter.

- Talking About Letters and Sounds, pages 77, 78
- Talking About Letter Shapes and Sounds, page 79
- Talking About Letter Sounds and Patterns, page 80
- Decoding and Interpreting the Structure of Words, page 89

A number of STRETCH charts explore the phonetic principle that letters have some relationship to speech sounds. Students talk about the beginning, medial, and final consonants and sounds, and the rhymes of words. They learn letter names, shapes, and sounds, beginning with highly contrasting sounds. These STRETCH charts familiarize students with word knowledge such as the establishment of consonant sound associations and blends. Use these STRETCH charts to highlight the structural components of words. Some prompts explore meaning of words according to the structure of the word.

Conventions of Print Strategies

- Talking About Print, page 81
- Interpreting Conventions of Print, page 90

Use these STRETCH charts to examine the components of print — the concepts of words, spaces, and letters. Students learn that letters may be written in upper case and lower case and in different styles of print. They highlight the punctuation conventions, the phonetic principles (the idea that letters have some relationship to speech sounds), and consistency principle (same word has same spelling).

Talking about the conventions of print teaches students how good readers assume the important role of text decoder.

Grammar Strategies

- Talking About Words, page 82
- Interpreting Grammar, page 91

Use these STRETCH charts so your students become familiar with the special features of how written dialect is organized and sequenced. Syntax or grammatical structures are learned through meaningful examination of them in a whole text, not through worksheets. Introduce your students to increasingly complex sentences and the conventions of direct speech and indirect speech, including the shift from present to past tense, and from first and second person to third using the pronoun. Also engage them in the interpretation of the structures and conventions of literary language. Talking about grammar teaches students how good readers assume the important role of text user.

Expression Strategies

- Talking About Expression, page 83
- Interpreting Expression, page 92

Students get practice in fluency and expression with practice time in audience reading.

Use these STRETCH charts to make your students familiar with intonation patterns for different kinds of texts. You want them to use vocabulary formally and dramatize their speech appropriately as part of their growth with functional language. You want them to be able to select the appropriate expression for a particular context or occasion, and be able to punctuate their voice with intonation from clues such as sentence form, punctuation, patterns, italics, capitalization, and bold face. There are few visual clues to stress and pitch, so this is a particularly difficult task for some students. They need practice with juncture, the significant pauses or breaks in the flow of the speech. They experiment with mood, atmosphere, pace, rhythm, and tension of language. Talking about expression teaches students how good readers assume the important role of text user.

Genre Strategies

- Interpreting Genre, page 93

This STRETCH chart makes your students familiar with a variety of different registers and gives them the ability to shift register when appropriate. They engage in a continuing discussion of the criteria for the right word for the context and occasion. Use this STRETCH chart so they will be aware of how to change the language level for different purposes. They also learn about words that may not be commonly used in conversation. Talking about genre teaches students how good readers assume the important role of text user.

Contextual Strategies

- Talking About Context, page 84
- Interpreting Word Context, page 95

Use these STRETCH charts to make your students familiar with the context clues to determine meaning, including new and multiple meanings. Word order and grammatical form, or syntactical clues, also contribute to this understanding. Some definitions are available within the context and some are determined by semantic clues or sentence meanings. Talking about context clues teaches students how good readers assume the important role of text user.

Comprehension Strategies

- Talking About the Meaning of Text, page 85
- Interpreting Meaning, pages 95, 96

Use these STRETCH charts to extend students' vocabulary beyond their current reading level. Mixing conversation and reading is an ideal way to anchor new words into a known context, rather than in isolation. Students develop a fascination for the sounds of words and, where appropriate, the simple relatives of words and multiple meanings. They use this involvement to examine the meaning of the text. Talking about comprehension teaches students how good readers assume the important role of text user.

Critical Literacy Strategy

- Interpreting Text Critically, page 97

Use this STRETCH chart to assist students in determining the author's theme, message, or point of view. Students learn the awareness readers need to understand the wider message conveyed through a particular text. They can determine, together, what might be some of the fundamental purposes of a text and the bias of the author. They can gain a growing awareness of the subtle influence of personal perspective or purpose. They can determine what is important and unimportant, and the impressions and generalizations that can be made. Use these prompts to help them recognize techniques of persuasion and propaganda. Talking about the critical interpretation of text teaches students how good readers assume the important role of text user.

Writer's Strategies

- Examining the Writer's Discovery of Subject, page 98
- Examining the Writer's Sense of Audience, pages 99, 100
- Examining the Writer's Tone, page 101
- Examining the Writer's Search for Specifics, page 102

Use this important series of STRETCH charts to familiarize students with the precious particles of good writing. The prompts lead to discussions of what techniques good writers use to make a good story, so that student writers can engage in a good understanding of the complex business of writing. Talking about the writer's strategies shows students how good writers assume the important role of text analyst to deepen their understanding of how to write well.

Primary STRETCH Chart:
Talking About Feelings and Attitudes

Aesthetic Strategy: Good readers think about the pictures they imagine, the feelings, and the attitudes they have when reading.

Code and talk about a word, phrase, or sentence that helps you respond to

- a person word; proper name, improper
- a person that reminds you of someone you know, of yourself
- a person who seems real or life like to you
- a person who is unreal or does not seem real to you
- something important to you
- something that made you think of something that happened to you
- something you find interesting
- something you did not react the same way to
- something you would like to be, you would not like to be
- something that you feel strongly about
- something you do not agree with, you do not understand
- something you do not find interesting
- something that makes you laugh, that makes you cry
- something you would like to share with your shoulder partner
- something that is boring to you
- something you would like to draw
- something that makes you think of a special food, color, shape, line

Code and talk about a word, phrase or sentence that

- you like
- interests you
- is a favorite
- you admire
- is a problem
- reminds you of something
- reminds you of someone
- concerns you
- confuses you
- you wish to comment on
- you have a strong opinion on
- you have a question about
- you would like to remember
- is your least favorite
- you will think about again
- you want to find out more about
- pleases you
- offends you

Primary STRETCH Chart:
Talking About Our Thinking

Metacognitive Strategy: Good readers think about their thinking when they read.

Code and talk about a word, phrase, or sentence that

- you have prior knowledge of, or you knew right away
- you looked at the picture for help with
- you figured out from the word clues around the difficult word (context)
- you predicted or guessed about
- gave you a clue about what was coming next in the text
- you actively solved, was tricky to solve
- you knew you weren't paying attention to
- is important to you
- you see often, you don't see often
- you went back and reread
- changed your reading speed
- made you thinking about what you know
- was unknown to you
- made pictures in your mind
- made you ask for help
- made you access your previous experiences, knowledge, feelings
- made you think of a time when…
- was punctuation you followed
- made you scan the text to look for specific information

Code and/or tell about

- a strategy a good speller would use
- a strategy that helped you learn a new word
- part of the text you self-monitored your own understanding of
- part of the text you did not understand
- a strategy you used to figure a word you didn't know
- a word that stands out for you, and why
- a part that drew you in as a reader
- a part that gives a clear and vivid picture in your mind
- a part that you had to break apart and put back together in order to read it
- a part that seems irrelevant
- when you had to look at the words around a part to figure it out
- a part that makes you want to read on

Primary STRETCH Chart:
Talking About Letters and Sounds

Phonological Strategy: Good readers think about their letters and sounds in words and the parts of words.

Code and talk about these words or letters:

- (letters) consonants that are the good guys; they talk
- (letters) consonants that are the tough guys; they don't talk
- letters that are called vowels
- words that rhyme with… (log, cat, toy, girl, lamp, look, desk, mutt, drink, red, green, bike, mouse, ball, socks, shirt)
- two words that end in a _____ sound (say the sound) and one that does not have this sound
- two words that begin with the same sound as _____ and one that does not begin with this sound
- words you can take the first letter off and still have a word (say the word with the first letter, say the word without the first letter)
- words you blend together to make a new word
- words that have this sound at the beginning of the word: _____
- words you can take some off the beginning of and still have a word
- a word that has two letters at the beginning that make one sound
- a word that has three letters at the beginning that make one sound
- a word that has a little word in the bigger word (neat/eat, pink/ink, soften/often)
- a word you can add a letter to the beginning of to make a new word
- a word you can add a new letter to and make a new word
- a word where you can mix the letters up and make a new word

Primary STRETCH Chart:
Talking About Letters and Sounds

Phonological Strategy: Good readers think about the letters and sounds in words and the parts of words.

Code and talk about a word that

- has a letter you know
- you had to match to the print
- begins with m, s, k, t
- begins with bl, fl, pl, sl, st
- begins with br, cr, dr, fr, gr, tr, str
- begins with sm, sn, sw, pr, cl, gl, tw, kn, wr, sp, spr, sh, ph, ch, th
- you ear spell (sounds right)
- you eye spell (looks right)
- has a silent letter
- has the letter _____ at the beginning
- has the letter _____ at the end
- has the letter _____ in the middle
- has bl, cl, dr
- has au, ou, oo, oi
- rhymes
- has a letter that is in your name
- has s, ed, ing, es, er
- has the prefix be-
- is important
- has one syllable, two syllables, three syllables, _____ syllables
- is a high-frequency word
- has _____ letters
- has double letters
- has letter clusters (e.g., tion)
- has unusual letters
- has a little word in a big word

Primary STRETCH Chart:
Talking About Letter Shapes and Sounds

Phonological Strategy: Good readers think about the shape and sound of letters and the parts of words when they read and write.

Code and talk about

- a letter you know already
- a tall letter
- a short letter
- a letter with circles
- a letter with tunnels
- a letter with a tail
- a letter with a dot
- a letter with a cross through it
- a letter you see often
- a letter you don't see very often
- a double letter
- a letter with a capital
- a lower case letter
- a consonant
- a vowel (a, e, i, o, u)
- a favorite letter
- a word with a letter from your name
- a letter that you know

- a letter that is hard for you
- a letter that makes a sound you like
- a letter that makes several sounds
- a sound that different pairs of letters make
- letters that often go together
- a fun letter
- a tricky letter
- consonants m, s, k, t
- blends bl, fl, pl, sl, st, br, cr, dr, fr, gr, tr, str
- ch, sh, th, wh (digraphs)
- st, sp, sn, sm, sl, sc, sk, sw, pr, cl, gl, tw, kn, wr, sp, spr
- fl, gl, pl, br, cr, dr, fr, pr, tr
- spl, str, spr, scr, squ
- ll, ss, ff, ck

Primary STRETCH Chart:
Talking About Letter Sounds and Patterns

Phonological Strategy: Good readers think about the shape and sound of letters and the patterns in words when they read and write.

Code and talk about (and add to the Word Wall) words with:

- tch, ch
- -age
- -tion
- -ture
- -ic
- -le
- silent letters mb, gh, kn, wr
- le
- dge
- ture
- a_e, ai, ay, ei, ea
- _e, ea, ee, y, ey, ie
- y, i_e, igh, ie
- ck, ke, nk, ng

- hard and soft c
- hard and soft g
- kn, wr, ight
- ph, gh
- _o, oa, o_e, ow, oe
- u_e, oo, ew, ue, ou, ui
- ou, ow (out, how)
- oo (good, look, foot)
- oi, oy
- ar, or, er, ir, ur, air, are, ear
- nk
- ng
- ck, ke
- dge, ge

Primary STRETCH Chart:
Talking About Print

Conventions of Print Strategy: Good readers and writers think about the conventions of print to help them read and write.

Code and talk about

- an upper case letter or capital letter
- a lower case letter or small letter
- your favorite letter
- bold face
- an underlined word
- emphasized text
- quotation marks, talking marks
- the beginning of an important part
- the end of a sentence
- the beginning of a sentence
- first, last word in a paragraph
- a space
- a punctuation mark (. , ! ? # @ $ ^ & ( ) [ ] \ ' " ")
- punctuation you would change
- what shows where a paragraph starts
- what you would edit
- a proofreading mistake

- a joining word (and, but, how)
- synonyms: the same
- antonyms: opposite
- homonyms: sound alike
- something abbreviated
- something small, medium, or large
- an ending; suffix (-ly, -y, -er, -ing, -s, -ed, -er, -est, -y, -tor, -ies, -or, -ied, -ation, -ture, -ness, -ment, -ous, -ic, ish)
- a contraction
- something that is next in alphabetical order
- a root word
- a prefix (dis-, re-)
- something not often seen
- something that is difficult to say

Primary STRETCH Chart:
Talking About Words

Grammar Strategy: Good readers and writers think about the way words are organized and sequenced.

Code and talk about

- a person word
- a place word
- a thing word
- an adjective tells what kind or how many
- a pronoun
- an action word
- a descriptive word
- a word for something you can touch
- a word for something you cannot touch
- adding a noun (e.g., find pronoun *he*, write the noun it refers to)
- changing a noun (e.g., find noun *cat*, change to *feline*)
- a preposition (e.g., *at*)
- a joining word (e.g., *and, or, but, either…or, because, when, unless*)
- adding a verb (e.g., find word *snake*, write word *slither*)
- changing a verb (e.g., find word *jump*, write word *leap)*
- adding an adjective (e.g., find word *snake*, write words *scaly, long*)
- changing an adjective (e.g., find word *skinny*, write word *thin*)
- adding a plural ending
- an irregular verb (am-was-been, begin-began-begun, bleed-bled-bled, choose-chose-chosen, do-did-done, fly-flew-flown)
- a possessive noun (e.g., *boy's*)
- an interjection or strong or sudden emotion (e.g., *Ugh!*, *Bravo!*)

Primary STRETCH Chart:
Talking About Expression

Expression Strategy: Good readers use expression when reading a text.

Code and talk about a word, phrase, or sentence

- that should be read quietly
- that needs an excited voice
- with a different voice (e.g., mysterious, musical, robotic, spiritual)
- with a changed speed
- that needs action in your voice
- in a way to make it sound more interesting
- that is you favorite part to say
- that the author might like to say
- with a narrator's voice with sound tracking (using sounds to create a mood/sense of place)

Primary STRETCH Chart:
Talking About Context

Contextual Strategy: Good readers use the context to figure out words.

Code and talk about a word that

- is what the whole text is about
- is a part or detail of the text
- was hard to read, and now is easy to read
- you guessed from the rest of the text
- you didn't know before
- is explained in a phrase following the word
- adds detail to the text
- is a definition within the context

Primary STRETCH Chart:
Talking About the Meaning of Text

> **Comprehension Strategy:** Good readers take time to interpret the meaning of the text.

Code and talk about a word, phrase, or sentence that

- tells what the story is about
- tells what the writer is saying
- tells what the illustrator is saying
- is like another word you know
- has a word within a word
- is the main idea
- is a detail
- tells the message or moral of the story
- you can web the meaning of
- tells what is going on
- you can say in your own words
- tells what is going to happen next
- tells about something that has already happened
- could happen to you
- you can add a word to without changing the meaning
- you can paraphrase
- you have a question about
- could not happen to you
- you could change to make more interesting
- you question

Intermediate STRETCH Chart:
Interpreting Images, Feelings, and Attitudes About the Text

> **Aesthetic Strategy:** Good readers pay attention to the images, feelings, and attitudes that surface when they read.

Code and talk about a word, phrase, or sentence that helps you respond to

- a person word; proper name, improper
- a person that reminds you of someone you know
- a person who reminds you of yourself
- a person who seems real or life-like to you
- a person who is unreal or does not seem real to you
- something important to you
- something that made you think of something that happened to you
- something you find interesting
- something you did not react to the same way
- something you would like to be
- something you would not like to be
- something that you feel strongly about
- something that pleases you
- something that offends you
- something that confuses you
- something you do not agree with
- something you do not understand
- something you do not find interesting

- something that makes you laugh
- something that makes you cry
- something that makes you remember something
- something you would like to share with your shoulder partner
- something that is boring to you
- something you would like to draw
- something you would like to share with someone who is not in this class
- something that makes you think of a special food
- something that makes you think of a special color
- something you associate with warm or cold colors
- something you associate with a square shape
- something you associate with a wavy lines

Intermediate STRETCH Chart:
Interpreting Images, Feelings, and Attitudes About the Text

> **Aesthetic Strategy:** Good readers pay attention to the images, feelings, and attitudes that surface when they read.

Code and talk about a word, phrase, or sentence that

- you like
- interests you
- is a favorite
- you admire
- is a problem
- reminds you of something
- reminds you of someone
- concerns you
- confuses you
- you wish to comment on
- you have a strong opinion on
- you have a question about
- you would like to remember
- is your least favorite
- you will think about again
- you want to find out more about
- pleases you
- offends you

Intermediate STRETCH Chart:
Interpreting Our Thinking Strategies

Metacognitive Strategy: Good readers think about their thinking when they read and write.

Code and talk about a word, phrase, or sentence that

- you have prior knowledge of, or you knew right away
- you figured out from the word clues around the difficult word
- you predicted or guessed about
- gave you a clue about what was coming next in the text
- helped you learn a new word
- you actively solved, is tricky to solve
- distracted you from the text
- you knew you weren't paying attention to
- is important to you
- you see often
- you went back and reread
- you went back and reread after going ahead
- changed your reading speed
- made you think about what you know
- was unknown to you, made you self-monitor your own understanding
- made pictures in your mind
- made you ask for help
- made you access your previous experiences, knowledge, feelings
- made you think of a time when…
- made you follow punctuation
- made you scan the text to look for specific information

Code and/or tell about

- a strategy a good speller would use
- part of the text you self-monitored your own understanding of
- part of the text you did not understand
- a strategy you used to figure a word you didn't know
- what helped you learn a new word
- a part you went back to reread after going ahead
- a word that stands out for you, and why
- a part that drew you in as a reader
- a part that gives a clear and vivid picture in your mind
- a part that you had to break apart and put back together in order to read it
- a part that seems irrelevant
- when you had to look at the words around a part to figure it out
- a part that makes you want to read on

Intermediate STRETCH Chart:
Decoding and Interpreting the Structure of Words

Phonological Strategy: Good readers and writers think about the sounds, structures, and meanings of words.

Code and talk about a word that

- is a compound word
- is a contraction
- has a prefix (dis-, com-, pre-, mis-, con-, pro-, re-)
- has a suffix (-s, -ed, -er, -ation, -tion, -(b)le, -ty, -ly, -able, -ness, -ment, -ous, -ing, -est, -ic, -ish)
- starts with a vowel and ends with a vowel
- starts with a consonant and ends with a consonant
- is borrowed from French
- has a Latin roots (act, anima, aqua, nat, port, san, terr)
- has Greek roots (aero, geo, gram, ortho, ped, therm, saur)
- has no meaning on its own
- is abbreviated
- is a high-frequency word
- has more than 6, 7, 8, 9 letters
- has less than four letters
- is the same spelled backwards

Intermediate STRETCH Chart:
Interpreting Conventions of Print

Conventions of Print Strategy: Good readers and writers think about the conventions of print to help them read and write.

Code and talk about

- bold face
- an underlined word
- emphasized text
- quotation marks, talking marks
- the beginning of an important part
- the end of a sentence
- the beginning of a sentence
- first, last word in a paragraph
- a space
- a punctuation mark
  (. , ! ? # @ $ ^& ( ) [ ] \ ' " ")
- punctuation you would change
- what shows where a paragraph starts
- what you would edit
- a proofreading mistake
- a joining word (and, but, how)
- synonyms: the same

- antonyms: opposite
- homonyms: sound alike
- something abbreviated
- something small, medium, or large
- an ending; suffix (-ly, -y, -er, -ing, -s, -ed, -er, -est, -y, -tor, -ies, -or, -ied, -ation, -ture, -ness, -ment, -ous, -ic, ish)
- a contraction
- something that is next in alphabetical order
- a root word
- a prefix (dis-, re-)
- something not often seen
- something that is difficult to say

Intermediate STRETCH Chart:
Interpreting Grammar

Grammar Strategy: Good readers and writers think about the way words are organized and sequenced.

Code and talk about

- a noun: person word
- a noun: place word
- a noun: thing word
- an adjective tells what kind or how many
- a pronoun
- a verb, action word
- an adverb, descriptive word
- a word for something you can touch
- a word for something you cannot touch
- adding a noun (e.g., find pronoun *she*, write word *dog* above)
- changing a noun (e.g., find word *dog*, change to *hound*)
- a preposition
- a conjunction, joining word
- a compound sentence
- adding a verb (e.g., find word *snake*, write word *slithering*)
- changing a verb (e.g., find word *slither*, write word *slide*)
- adding an adjective (e.g., find word *snake*, write words *scaly, long*)
- changing an adjective (e.g., find word *slimy*, write *gucky* above it)
- adding a plural ending
- an irregular verb (am-was-been, begin-began-begun, bleed-bled-bled, choose-chose-chosen, do-did-done, fly-flew-flown)
- a possessive noun
- an interjection

Intermediate STRETCH Chart:
Interpreting Expression

Expression Strategy: Good readers use expression when reading a text.

Code and talk about a word, phrase, or sentence

- that should be read quietly
- that needs an excited voice
- with a different voice (mysterious, musical, robotic, spiritual)
- with a changed speed
- that needs action in your voice
- in a way to make it sound more interesting
- that is you favorite part to say
- that the author might like to say
- with a narrator's voice with sound tracking (using sounds to create a mood/sense of place)

Intermediate STRETCH Chart:
Interpreting Genre

Genre Strategy: Good writers understand the relationship between the language and the context in which it is used, how writing serves a function in a particular context.

Code and talk about

- evidence of genre
- evidence that may not fit with this genre
- a word, phrase, sentence that fits with this genre
- a part that confuses the genre
- a place where missing text could be placed
- conventions of print that fit with this genre
- specific genre characteristics
- a part that you like
- the main idea of this genre
- words closest to the theme
- a part that reminds you of another genre like this
- words that invoke feelings
- words that are tied to the present, past, or future
- words that you appreciate
- what gives you factual information
- what gives you fictional information
- what you would change

Intermediate STRETCH Chart:
Interpreting Word Context

Contextual Strategy: Good readers use the context to understand the meaning of words.

Code and talk about a word that

- is what the whole text is about
- is a part or detail of the text
- was hard to read, and now is easy to read
- you guessed from the rest of the text
- you didn't know before
- is explained in a phrase following the word
- adds detail to the text
- is a definition within the context

Intermediate STRETCH Chart:
Interpreting Meaning

Comprehension Strategy: Good readers take the time to interpret the meaning of the text.

Code and talk about a word, phrase, or sentence that

- tells what the story is about
- tells what the writer is saying
- tells what the illustrator is saying
- is like another word you know
- has a word within a word
- is the main idea
- is a detail
- tells the message or moral of the story
- you can web the meaning of
- tells us what is going on
- you can say in your own words
- tells what is going to happen next
- tells about something that has already happened
- could happen to you
- you can add a word to without changing the meaning
- you can paraphrase
- you have a question about
- could not happen to you
- you could change to make more interesting
- you question

- you have prior knowledge of
- you can paraphrase information about
- is something you can see
- is something you could not see
- shows cause and effect
- compares
- contrasts
- shows denotation
- shows connotation
- shows metaphor
- you will remember
- represents something significant in the story

Intermediate STRETCH Chart:

Interpreting Meaning

Comprehension Strategy: Good readers interpret the meaning of text.

Code and talk about a word, phrase, or sentence:

Knowledge

- you can recall
- you can recognize
- you can identify
- who, what, where, when

Comprehension

- a word you can describe
- a word you can make a comparison with
- a word you can interpret
- a phrase you can rephrase
- a word you can contrast
- a word you can explain
- a word that gives the main idea

Application

- you can apply to your own life
- you can classify
- you will use

Intermediate STRETCH Chart:
Interpreting Text Critically

Critical Literacy Strategy: Good readers are critical in their interpretation of a text.

Code and talk about a word, phrase, or sentence that you think

- should be the title of the story
- should have happened
- should be different
- is the topic
- is the theme
- is part of the discourse being used
- expresses the voices and positions of the text
- shows what the text trying to do to you
- is what wasn't said about the topic; why?
- are the voices and positions not being expressed
- is bias of the author
- is the perspective taken
- is the author's purpose, motive
- had be left out, unsaid
- has been said
- is how the author handled the selection
- is important
- is not important
- counters opposing conclusions you may have
- is sales talk
- is advertising jargon (such as "magic", or "enchanting")
- is a quotation out of context
- is name-calling
- is unsupported generalization
- is a biased selection of items
- appeals to authority (famous person who uses product)
- is a misleading headline

Intermediate STRETCH Chart:
Examining the Writer's Discovery of Subject

Writer's Strategy: Good writers discover their subject.

Code and talk about a part of the text that

- is the one important topic, worthwhile (just one in the story?)
- moves to action fast
- shows "what"
- gives the reader something
- shows the author knows, cares about it, looks inward, loves
- exposes the author, shows author "with the skin off" or vulnerable
- frames a beginning (situation, set up; clear, safe tone; hint of a character; who, what, where)
- frames a middle (problem)
- frames an end (resolve)
- creates order
- shows a relationship, pattern, connections
- shows focus, focus, focus
- takes away from the focus
- is another possible topic, could be used for another piece (is there a mini-story?)
- really gets it right, is carefully crafted
- floods, gives a feel for the moment
- indicates a habit of observation
- shares a measure of disturbance, a need to be understood
- is a lead, topic sentence that teaches us how to read the text, tells us what it is about
- is a lead that starts with action, carefully sets up what will happen
- makes you feel safe about where you, the reader, are
- has small specifics that set the tone
- is a hint of mystery
- is a hint about a character, dialogue that develops the characters

Intermediate STRETCH Chart:
Examining the Writer's Sense of Audience

Writer's Strategy: Good writers sense their audience.

Code and talk about a part of the text that communicates:

- promises what the story is about, telling reader what it is about
- gets to emotional truth
- brings themes to the universal
- is believable, rings true, you can buy it
- is not believable, does not ring true, you can't buy it
- brings you into the story as a reader

Code and talk about a part of the text that provides clarity and integrity:

- promises what the story is about, telling reader what it is about
- discovers the topic
- is believable, rings true, you can buy it
- is not believable, does not ring true, you can't buy it
- brings you into the story as a reader

Code and talk about a part of the text that looks inward:

- gives a belief of life
- indicates what the author is trying to do
- indicates a belief
- provides a real truth

Intermediate STRETCH Chart:
Examining the Writer's Sense of Audience

Writer's Strategy: Good writers sense their audience.

Code and talk about a part of the text that

- is not told, is inferred, doesn't spell things out, shows does not tell
- considers what the audience knows
- has marketability to _____
- is what would a _____ (person you write about) say about you, what you would say about them

Code and talk about a part of the text that has voice, tension, rhythm:

- gets the right voice, consistent overall impression
- rings true, you recognize it
- slows things down by writing more specifically
- moves the story along fast
- moves away from a strategic or dramatic point, for a moment
- presents a mystery (to be unraveled later)
- a situation of jeopardy
- a short sentence
- a long sentence
- a sentence that saves the best for last, has significant information at the end of it

Intermediate STRETCH Chart:
Examining the Writer's Tone

Writer's Strategy: Good writers set the tone of the story.

Code and talk about a part of the text that

- is personable, has likeability
- makes the reader feel, think they are intelligent
- forges a relationship
- anticipates the reader's needs
- is attentive
- provides modest humbleness
- asks a question, talks to the reader to make it friendly
- indicates sympathy or caring
- projects warmth and emotion, talks about how the author feels
- persuades with examples, not opinion

Code and talk about the start of the story that communicates through a

- character
- setting
- plot (e.g., The front door slammed.)
- dialogue that moves the story forward
- flashback
- letter, newspaper
- statement of philosophy
- prologue (must be important to the story)

Intermediate STRETCH Chart:

Examining the Writer's Search for Specifics

Writer's Strategy: Good writers search for specifics for their writing.

Code and talk about a part of the text that

- indicates research
- shows, doesn't tell
- matters, has interesting details
- has details that don't matter (the writer may want to get rid of these)
- has words that don't have purpose (the writer may want to get rid of these)
- has words that have a purpose
- is authentic
- looks inward
- is convincing, has a visceral feeling
- appeals to the senses, brings it alive through the senses
- takes an implicative stance, implies things
- indicates motion, examples of movement or lack of movement
- has sound
- has something specific, something universal
- provides emotional flooding
- provides something the reader needs to know
- tells something you think the reader didn't need to know
- is overwritten
- characterizes, or develops information, too late in the story
- has ineffective description (the writer may want to get rid of this)
- has effective description
- has transitions
- counts, does its job

Code and talk about part of the text that could be edited through

- tightening up (saying it in a phrase)
- taking it out
- changing an unnecessary sentence, clause

Composite STRETCH Chart

Strategy: _____

Code and talk about a word, phrase, or sentence that

_____

_____

_____

Strategy: _____

Code and talk about a word, phrase, or sentence that

_____

_____

_____

Strategy: _____

Code and talk about a word, phrase, or sentence that

_____

_____

_____

Strategy: _____

Code and talk about a word, phrase, or sentence that

_____

_____

_____

Chapter 6: Independent Centres

Independent centres make up the last important strategy of an extensive, best-practice vocabulary instruction program that will make words stick in the minds of young readers.

Centres provide the time to take the words that have become familiar to students during the read-aloud/picture study and shared reading, and continue the systematic instruction in pragmatics, syntax, semantics, and graphophonics. Whole-to-parts phonics instruction teaches the parts of the words after the story has been read "to" (read aloud) and "with" (shared reading) the children. At centres the reading is done independently "by" the children.

In centres, children learn to enjoy books and stories through time to appreciate the rewards of print. They participate in extensive, repetitive experiences with a wide range of favorite books. They learn more about multiple ways to pronounce given letters and strings of letters, multiple meanings, and usages. They analyze a variety of word families to increase their structural level of understanding. They increase the number of words that they read and spelled automatically. They practise strategies for handling written language.

Reading Centres

The read-aloud context has provided students with explicit, direct instruction of new vocabulary and what it means to be a good reader and writer. The shared reading context has provided them with guided practice in conversation about what good readers and writers do. Independent centres afford students time to perform as self-initiating readers. Students learn how to

- be independent
- value their individual personal best
- behave responsibly
- acknowledge individual differences
- acknowledge differentiated learning
- benefit from differentiated learning
- play with words, reading, writing, and representing
- perform as good readers, writers, listeners, and speakers

Daily Reading

Stanovich (1998) estimated that Grade 5 students who did independent reading read 622,000 more words than those who did not.

As part of a comprehensive vocabulary system, have students read independently each day. Word learning opportunities begin with significant amounts of reading. Our students have between 15 and 30 minutes to read at the independent reading centre each day. Some days they read alone at a recreational reading level and other days they read collaboratively with a buddy or in a small group.

Writing Centres

The more sharing you do of what you go through as you write, the more effective you will be at helping students become writers. The more talking you do about what you go through as a writer, the more effective readers, writers, listeners, and speakers you will all likely become.

You can create a powerful guided writing centre by giving the act of writing (Murray, 1968) as much importance as the text that comes out of the writing. Use this centre to talk in a small group about the struggles and successes you have when you are writing. Try to share your thoughts and feelings on what you were thinking as you composed and read what you write.

Encourage students to understand that there are no absolute rules about composing text, but there are many things we need to think about and need to work on. Remind them that this strategy will help them discover many of the components of good writing and how to use them to become successful writers (Murray, 1968).

Students need time to discover the topics that matter most to them. They have deep and personal reasons to write and many stories to tell. Most of the stories and poems they produce, however, are approximations of adult text. They are less than perfect by conventional adult writing standards. Use centre time to mediate this complex process as students go through individual and collaborative writing conferences. New personal vocabulary knowledge is cultivated through giving students choice, creativity, and voice in the writing they do during centre time.

Word-Play and Representing Centres

Word-play centres continue students' engagement in the systematic inquiry of vocabulary. One of the best ways to create a positive environment for vocabulary development is through word-play centres. Students love to be challenged to classify and organize words into special lists, Word Wall categories, or graphic organizers. These kinds of open-ended activities can be highly motivating for many literacy learners. Word play is an especially useful way to engage at-risk, low-progress students into participating in literacy.

We use the representing centre as another opportunity for students to represent their vocabulary development. Four centres provide for smaller group sizes and more opportunities to differentiate the learning. In the representing centre, students continue to work with the same kinds of challenges that are set out in the word-play centre, but this centre has the flexibility to set out unique representing challenges as well. The representing centre allows you the flexibility to provide any number of literacy activities to best meet the needs of the diverse group of students. There are activities described in Chapter 7 that can be used in either word-play or representing centres.

Accomplishments of Word-Play Centres

Motivational Accomplishments
- enjoy a variety of genres
- appreciate the rewards of print
- have extensive experiences with print
- have repetitive experiences with print

Linguistic Accomplishments
- work creating genres and special features of text
- work with vocabulary
- work with intonation patterns
- work with idioms

Operational Accomplishments
- self monitor strategies: self-correcting, confirmation, cross-checking strategies
- predict words: use context to fill in unknown words
- structural operations: follow sequence, events, plots, arrangements of letters, words, sentences

Orthographic Accomplishments
- understand print
- directional conventions: front to back of book, left to right, top of page to bottom, end of line sweep
- print components: words, spaces, letters
- letter form generalization: upper case, lower case, styles and sizes of print
- punctuation conventions
- phonetic principles: letter shape, sound
- consistency principle: same word has same spelling

Choose activities to give your students the means to represent their thinking in ways that match their strengths. Also try to encourage them to stretch themselves by thinking in modes that they are not as strong in.

Context: *Independent Centres*
Text: *Scarecrow by Cynthia Rylant, range of books and other reading and writing material*
Important Concept Words: *wonder, witness, real, mammoth, borrowed*
Strategy: *Individual Graphic Organizers, Independent Word Play*
Level of Instruction: *Self-directed, student-centred learning*
Grouping: *Individual/small group/ teacher-guided reading group*

During centres, students participate in four different small-group activities. These centres are designed to further anchor their key vocabulary and challenge them to become independent in their use of reading strategies. With each centre, the students have another pass at challenges that make words stick. I strategically design the representing and word-play centres to relate to the read-aloud/picture study, so that I can effectively take the third pass at exposing my students to key vocabulary.

Centres

Group 1	Group 2	Group 3	Group 4
Writing	Word Play	Representing	Reading
Word Play	Representing	Reading	Writing
Representing	Reading	Writing	Word Play
Reading	Writing	Word Play	Representing

Independent Word-Play Centre

We decided as a class during shared reading that there are many compounds words in the *Scarecrow* shared reading text. I decide to make the independent word-play centre a compound-word challenge. The students make a list of compound words on the chalkboard. They work in partners to create compound words in big print to share with the class. The challenge is to list compound words from the shared reading text and then go to other resources for the rest of the words. We review that good writers look in dictionaries, use thesauruses, or even ask others. The first group's list of compound words looks like this:

scare / crow
under / stand
some / body
ten / foot / tall
for / ever
wit /ness

I see the potential for a mini-lesson when I observe this group. They have listed the word wit / ness. At the end of centre time, we can discuss why or why not witness is a compound word. We will share their favorite words from the list, so there is an audience for the sharing of their meaning-making and accountability.

Reading Centre

I use a variety of levels of vocabulary instruction during centres. I have the flexibility to work at a high level of support with guided reading groups to further develop their independent use of word recognition strategies. There is a low level of support with the rest of the students participating independently in their student-centred cooperative learning groups. If everyone is working independently, I can work with the guided reading group on the *Scarecrow* shared reading text we did in the morning. It is of great benefit to most students to revisit, reread, and relearn about the text again in the comfort of the small-group guided reading lesson. We decide to rehearse our knowledge of what good readers do when they come to a word they do not know. We think about the shared reading text and talk about the strategies we used to be good readers. We share this information with the others at the end of this centre time.

It is valuable to observe the students during the shared reading lesson to assess the new level of understanding of their targeted words.

Writing Centre

The writing centre is where we test our skills at witnessing and wondering. I have chosen to put some snails safely in a terrarium in front of the students. I challenge them to make a semantic map of the words, phrases, or sentences that best describes their "noticings," their witnessing and wondering about the life of the snails. I remind them of the scarecrow's witnessing of life, and encourage them to have "long, slow, scarecrow thoughts" about what they see. The students may choose to work collaboratively to map their words as a prewriting for narrative or poetry. I provide jewellers' eyeglasses, or loupes, to magnify the snails for my students' first-hand witnessing and wondering. We will share their mapping of words at the conclusion of this centre.

Representing Centre

One group of six students has been given the semantic map from the *Scarecrow* read-aloud and they are choosing words from it to make a list of relationships. Quoting "His hat has housed mice and his arms have rested birds," I challenge the students to think carefully about the relationship of the hat as a house for a mouse or arms as a house for the birds. I suggest to them that my arms could be a house for one of them or for my cat Chewbacca. They agree to try to think of some ideas of their own:

- Straw is a house for a napping barn cat.
- A jacket is a house for a scarecrow.
- A cave is a house for a bat.
- A class is a house for a chalkboard.
- A book is a house for words.

I encourage the students to take some time to illustrate each of their ideas. They will get to share their favorite idea and picture at the conclusion of the centre time. Each new group will be able to read what the group before them has done, and to add their own new ones to it.

The Centres Approach

Independence

Nurturing our vocabulary learners' own independent reflective inquiry and exploration of words is critical to their literacy success. We want them to ask "how" and "why" words work the way they do. We want them to be aware of words, be interested in words, and effectively use reading and writing strategies. With centres, we invite students to personally inquire about a much greater variety of word meanings. We prepare centre activities that give students differentiated, independent learning opportunities to play with the words they need to know, including a variety of key utility and personal words.

Differentiated Learning

Students are more involved, engaged, and confident when they participate in activities tailored to their individual needs.

We conceptualize independent centres as a large block of time to differentiate the learning tasks for our students. In each of the four centres, the reading, writing, word play, and representing are designed to meet the students' individual needs, styles, and interests. One-size centres will not fit all.

A centres approach allows you to differentiate the content, skills, and strategies you teach students. Change the pace, level, and tasks of the centres they attend. Give out specific challenges to partners or individuals at the word-play centre. Give them access to resources that match their current level of understanding. Personalize the centres, providing additional instruction or extended learning experiences to meet individual needs. As the teacher, you are freed up to decide what students you will work with while other students work independently. You can affirm, appreciate, and acknowledge individual differences during this time.

Differentiated Vocabulary Instruction

In order to make sense of a whole text, readers have to first become efficient at recognizing individual words with as little effort as possible. Centres give students specific independent word challenges to ensure that they are able to associate the letters and groups of letters with sounds and blend them into syllables and words.

Readers translate the written symbols that are grouped into words into their oral representation, hearing them in their head during silent reading. Centres give students specific independent word challenges to ensure that they are able to recognize familiar words easily and automatically.

Difficult, bigger words need to be recognized using a variety of techniques to decode them. Centres give students specific independent word challenges to ensure that they are able to see difficult and unfamiliar words, and to learn to use decoding skills to read them.

An important key to anchoring vocabulary development is ensuring that students with poor vocabularies not only learn the meanings of new words, but also have the opportunity to use them frequently. Both word-play and representing centres allow you the flexibility to give students differentiated challenges to work with specific kinds of words: to anchor words through lists of instant, utility words practised in isolation; to anchor words by using them in context; and to anchor words as an extension of the students' background knowledge. The key words are so important that they will need all of these strategies through all of the learning contexts.

Differentiate the methods, materials, and expectations in use for different students. You can differentiate the following components of the centre activities:

Vocabulary
- Simplicity of vocabulary
- Simplicity of syntax
- Density of new vocabulary
- Progressive repetition of vocabulary
- Memorable and meaningful language
- Language patterns
- Naturalness of the language

Prior Experience
- Familiarity with the activity
- Recency of exposure to the material
- Recency of experience

Personal Interest
- Intellectually interesting
- Aesthetically interesting
- Emotionally interesting
- Revisiting of an old favorite
- Social interest

Self-determination
- Choice of material
- Choice of pace of learning
- Choice of mode of representation

Purposefulness
- Related, situated in lives of students

Criteria of Centre Activity
- Size of project or activity
- Layout/format
- Materials used
- Medium to share
- Length of task
- Students involved

Sounds, Words to Play With
- phonogram manipulation
- sight words, words you want to become automatic
- word oddities
- stand-alones

Choose activities to give your students the means to represent their thinking in ways to match their strengths. Also try to encourage them to stretch themselves by thinking in modes that they are not as strong in.

Semantic clues: *satisfying meaning*

Syntactic predictions: *acceptable relationship of the words together*

Directional clues and positions: *from previous perceptual experiences*

Lexical and structural clues: *significant letters, letter clusters, affixes, roots, compounds*

Graphophonetic cues: *letter–sound association, expectations*

- instant words
- lists of frequently used words (color, numbers, theme)
- high-frequency words (was, saw, of, for, from, they, that, what, with, will)
- homophones
- synonyms
- homographs
- non-reversible words
- antonyms
- word origins
- key words from content areas
- word families
- similes
- strategies for working with words
- multiple meanings
- sentence structure
- anagram word play
- commonly misspelled words (they, were, could, was, where, does, come, said, pretty, of, because, people, from, have, again)
- Dolch Words (Edward Dolch, 1941)
- First 100 Instant Words
- action words
- really big words, so students chunk words or put letters together
- familiar patterns or little words to make bigger or new words (and–sand–stand)
- words with the same suffix
- word demons: words that have no meaning, are not spelled logically, and look a lot like each other

Principles of Best Practice in Centres

We develop a rich and supportive literacy-learning climate that matters to the teacher, the students, and their parents when we include these vital components to our independent centres:

- holistic teaching and developmental process learning
- experiential, active learning with a mixture of movement, talking, and sharing
- time devoted to reading on topics of personal choice and interest
- time devoted to writing on topics of personal choice and interest
- placing responsibility with the students for goal setting, assessment/evaluation
- enacting and modeling of democracy/ leadership roles
- attention to the various affective and cognitive styles of the students
- authentic cooperative collaborative learning
- classroom as a reflective interdependent community
- varied flexible groupings of students
- challenging students to higher levels of thinking, self-selected

Chapter 7: Using Centres

This chapter provides some brief explanation of worthwhile strategies that can be carried out in centres. All the strategies used are modeled or taught to the whole group so they have a good working knowledge of them before they proceed to use them independently. Samples of the activity sheets the students can use to focus their time at the centres are provided.

Reading Strategies

The theme of each reading centre is not a body of knowledge or information, but the attitudes and strategies of good readers. Promote the idea daily that students' efficiency with reading skills is achieved through the use of sound attitudes, understandings, and procedures — reading strategies. Endorse the following goals to develop their success with reading strategies:

- a fierce demand for meaning, for making the text make sense
- a spirit of independence, a willingness to "have a go"
- a confident use of helpful references: people, thesauruses, and dictionaries
- general procedures for word-attack and cross-checking strategies
- metacognition of the word-attack strategies being used

Partner Read Strategy

Strategy : Good readers use strategies to read hard words.

Use the Partner Read so students can improve their strategic reading of a text and reinforce their metacognition of their use of strategies. To do this, create a centre where students support each other in pairs as they read a text of their choice together.

We want our students to become aware of how to cue another student when they read. Using a Partner Read strategy encourages the students' active involvement in the monitoring of the reading of others with this simple cueing system:

1. Does it make sense?
2. Does it sound right?
3. Does it look right?

Each day one student presses their partner to use all three cueing systems when they are partner reading together.

Not only does the Partner Read strategy give students practice using their reading strategies independently, it also frees the you up to go around the room to assess and evaluate. You can assist students with improving their use of the strategy or note who needs more practice with a more expert partner, such as yourself or the learning assistant (likely at a scheduled time). You are now able to share the responsibility for the teaching and learning of important reading strategies with most of your students. You are able to provide intervention for those who need more scaffolding with their use of strategies.

Procedure: Partner Read
1. Sit in partners but read on your own.
2. Talk briefly about any words you have difficulty with. Get your partner to help if you get stuck on a word.
3. Talk together about what strategy you used to "have a go" at the hard word.
4. Look at the chart and decide what strategy you used to read the word.

We want our students to know what good readers do. Remind the students what they need to know by listing the strategies good readers use in the form of a chart. The students can refer to this chart as they read with their partner. This way, you make the strategies good readers use explicit to each of the students working at the reading centre.

Say It Fast Strategy

This independent centre also engages the students in improving their decoding of words. The Say It Fast strategy is designed to have students support each other in pairs as they take turns sharing some of the strategies they use to sound out words when they read. If students do not automatically know a word, they need to practise how to figure it out by taking some systematic steps. They look at the first letter, final letters, and middle letters. They look at the vowels, letter clusters, and small words in the larger words. Teach them how to take words apart, put them back together, and then say the parts from left to right very fast. Prompt them with "Say it fast!" Each day, the students practise, saying a list of words, decoding them, and saying them fast.

You also need to teach students that some words cannot be sounded out. There are words that that they just need to know. These words need to be recognized quickly, easily, and accurately. Familiar words need to be recognized automatically on sight, and practice with this makes perfect. Students need to learn that many words can be sounded out and many cannot, you just need to know them. Being explicit about the two kinds of words — eye-spelled words (the words you just look at and need to know) and ear-spelled words (the ones you can sound out to make sense of them) — is extremely helpful to some students as they make sense of reading.

Two Kinds of Words
Eye-spelled: you need to know by sight, cannot be sounded out
Ear-spelled: you can sound out to make sense of

Procedure: Say It Fast

1. Sit in partners with your list of words, text, or semantic map.
2. Talk briefly about any words you have difficulty with.
3. Get your partner to help you if you get stuck on a word.
4. Share how good readers look at the word and link the letters of each new word with the sound the word makes so they can say it.
5. Say the first word slowly, and think about how you say each part of the word.
6. Once you have looked and said the word slowly from beginning to end, have your partner cue you to "Say it fast!"

Recording the strategies that students use to read on a What Good Readers Do chart is an explicit way to remind them of the strategies to help them read.

Partner Prediction Strategy

This strategy gives students a chance to work with a partner guessing what will happen next in the text. A student can talk and share ideas with the partner. Many more students get to talk when they share the text this way. A student does not have to wait to share his ideas in front of 20–25 students, as would be necessary in whole-group teaching.

Procedure: Partner Prediction
One partner must decide ahead of time where to stop in the text and ask students to guess what comes next. Alternatively, the teacher can prepare the stops by placing sticky notes in the book for the students.

1. Work with you shoulder partner. You read the title and a few lines of text. You stop reading at the designated place (where the sticky note is located) and ask your partner to guess what will happen next in the text.
2. Discuss what he/she thinks will happen next.
3. You read a few lines so you can check the prediction.
4. You read a few more lines of text. You stop reading and ask your partner to guess what this next bit of text will be about.
5. You read a few lines to check the guess.
6. Shoulder partners continue in this manner with the rest of the story.

Silent Word Knowledge Support Strategy

This strategy is designed so that students support each another as they read.

Procedure: Silent Word Knowledge Support
1. Shoulder partners read the text silently.
2. You get help from one another in the reading of the text. Either of you may ask for help or share a question or comment with your partner.

- Group 1 is the girls in the class; group 2 is the boys in the class.
- Group 1 is students wearing black; group 2 is students wearing red.
- Groups can be selected based on birthdays, hair length, pets in family, etc.

Poetry Reading Strategy

There are many fun variations of this oral speaking strategy to actively involve four to six students in the reading of poetry. They can choral read a poem with everyone in the centre reading the poem in unison, or they can form into two groups with one group calling out the first line of poetry and the other group responding by saying the next.

Students also have fun copy-catting the poem with each other. One student in the group reads one line and the others repeat the same line when he/she is finished. Two students of the group may select to read one line, with the remaining students doing the copy-catting. Students love leading this activity, and become keen to choose the way to recite the poetry and decide which part they will have.

One of the more difficult forms of choral reading is reading for two or three voices. This requires the readers to synchronize the reading of different lines and sometimes read a line together. Poems can be adapted for two, three, or four voices. The leader is responsible for determining the suitability of the poem for this procedure. Select poetry books that have been written in this format or have the students take ordinary poems and adapt them to this style.

Singing poems is a hit at any grade level. A poem can be matched to song tunes that have the same meter. Simple songs like "Mary Had a Little Lamb," "Row, Row, Row, Your Boat," and "London Bridge" can be used for the singing of a poem. Beginning readers are encouraged through musical connections with poetry. They can remember these musical readings and return to sing them over and over again.

Procedure: Poetry Reading
1. Sit in a group and select the way to perform the poetry to the class.
2. Practise the performance.
3. Prepare an introduction of the poem to tell the class.

Variation
1. Two groups: one group stands, one group sits.
2. Group 1 (standing) reads line 1 standing up and then sits down.
3. Group 2 (sitting) stands up and reads line 2 and sits down.
4. Group 1 stands up and reads line 3 and sits down.
5. Group 2 stands up and reads line 4 and sits down.
The groups take turns until poem is finished.

Suggestions for Small Group Reading
- Poem is read aloud by author while others read along.
- Choral read: everyone reads together
- Popcorn read: anyone can read; jump in when you wish
- Echo read: one voice leads, other voices echo
- Poem is read aloud while students are drawing or making notations.
- Reading alone
- Line-a-child
- Line-a-group

- With partner quietly or silently
- Partner track: one partner reads while other student tracks, then switch

Just Read Strategy

This strategy is designed to give students time to just read at a recreational level. Reading is an effective strategy for students to develop vocabulary if they can use their increasing word knowledge to examine the words they read. They use this time to read material of their choice and interest with this in mind. They benefit from reading across a range of genres.

Readers Theatre Strategy

This strategy is designed for use with a text that has a number of different voices.

Procedure: Readers Theatre
1. Have your part assigned to you by a reading centre leader.
2. Sit in a circle and practise the readers theatre.
3. Read your parts as a readers theatre drama for the class.

Reading: Personal

Strategy: Good readers respond to their text.

1. Think about what you have read.
2. Use one of the prompts to help you.
3. Talk quietly about your ideas.

Prompts:
- I liked…
- I think…
- I noticed…
- I felt…
- I never knew…
- I never though…

Reading: Jump Rope Rhymes — Choral

Strategy: Good readers have fun with chants.

1. Read a Jump Rope Rhyme.
2. Chant it together.
3. Quietly practise your chant so that you can say it for the class.

Reading: Poetry

Strategy: Good readers have fun with words.

1. Read a poem.
2. Have your partner read the poem with you.
4. Repeat with other poems.
3. Pick two poems to share with the class.

Reading: The Important Thing About...

Strategy: Good readers think about the important things they want to say.

1. Think about what you think is **nice**.
2. Talk about what you think is important with your partner.
3. Write down in the form below what you think is important.

   Try one about **bad, sad, important, wonderful**.

The nice thing about _____ is _____

It _____

It _____

And it _____

But the nicest thing about _____ is _____

Reading: Tongue Twisters

Strategy: Good readers have fun with words.

1. Write down a tongue twister.
2. Have your partner say the tongue twister a few times fast.
3. Repeat with other tongue twisters.
3. Pick two to share with the class.

Some Tongue Twisters:

- Baboon bamboo
- Greek grapes
- She sells seashells by the seashore.
- Toy boat
- Three Free Throws
- Seven silly swans swam silently seaward.
- Six sick sheep
- A noisy noise annoys an oyster.

Reading: Jokes and Riddles

Strategy: Good writers have fun with words.

1. Write a joke or riddle.
2. Have your partner read the joke or riddle.
3. If it is a riddle, answer it.
4. Repeat with other jokes and riddles.
5. Pick two to share with the class.

Reading: 1 Minute Speeches/Stories

Strategy: Good readers read or retell short stories.

1. Read or retell a short story.
2. Practise reading it or retelling it.
3. Share it with the class.

Reading: Readers Theatre

Strategy: Good readers know lots of characters in a good story.

1. Sit in a circle, close together.
2. Pick your part.
3. Think about and practise your part.
4. Read the story together.
5. Share with the class.

Writing Strategies

Guided Writing Strategy

Strategy: Good writers share writing ideas.

Use this independent centre to engage the students in improving their strategic writing of a text. This strategy has students take turns sharing their struggles as writers.

Procedure: Shared Writing

1. Introduce yourself as a writer.
2. Share one piece of your writing and a part of your act of writing.
3. Talk briefly about what you were thinking when you wrote your piece.
4. Record this on a What Good Writers Do chart. Remind other students they might want to use this knowledge to help them with their writer.

Independent Writing Strategy

Strategy: Good writers recall, relate, and reflect.

Use an independent writing centre to have students write responses through retelling, relating, and/or reflecting upon one aspect of their learning (Schwartz and Bone, 1995). Provide prompts at the centre to assist the students in making their response.

Procedure: Good Readers and Writers Responding

1. Sit in partners.
2. Talk briefly about something you would like to retell, relate, or respond to.
3. Share your ideas using the recalling, relating, or responding prompts that follow.

Recalling is telling about _____ using your own words.

- I especially like…
- I noticed…
- I feel that…
- This is about…

Relating is the making of connections, the memories, the telling of personal stories.

- I remember…
- This reminds me of…
- This makes me think of…
- It's hard to believe…
- This makes me feel…

Reflecting is the wondering, the sharing of ideas and insights about

_____.

- Now I want to know…
- I wonder if…
- Now I understand…
- What do you think about…
- This gives me an idea to …

4. Talk together about what you will say.

Writing/Reading: Riddles

Strategy: Good readers/writers have fun with riddles.

1. Read or write a riddle from a riddle book.
2. Have your partner guess and write the answer.
3. Repeat with other riddles
4. Pick two to share with the class.

Writing: Good Handwriting

Strategy: Good writers make their letters and words carefully.

1. Practise making words carefully.
2. Check the letters carefully.
3. Say the words.
4. Close your eyes and picture the words.

Writing: Wiggle Words — Pantomime

Strategy: Good writers make pictures in the minds of their readers.

1. Write an action word.
2. Say the word.
3. Act out the word.
4. Close your eyes and picture the word in your mind.

Writing: Interest Inventory

Strategy: Good writers find out information before they write.

Sample Inventory

- **My favorite: color, food, toy, game, story, sport, TV show, person, day, season, place**
- **I like: to go, to learn, to read, to eat, to play**
- **Things I like to do: at home, at school, outside, inside, by myself, with friends**

1. Read the inventory.
2. Write down your ideas.
3. Write a story about YOU or the person you interview

Writing: Retell the Story

Strategies: Good writers have a good beginning, middle, and end to a story.

Good writers have a situation, problem, and resolution to their story.

Good writers have home–adventure–home parts to their story.

1. Fold your paper into four parts.
2. Write the title and author in the first box.
3. Draw in each box.
4. Write a sentence to go with each picture.

Story	Beginning	Middle	End

Story	Situation	Problem	Resolution

Story	Home	Adventure	Home

Writing: Spelling Demons

Strategy: Good spellers have a memory device or trick to remember hard words.

Sample Memory Device

  once = <u>o</u>nly <u>n</u>ice <u>c</u>ats <u>e</u>at

1. Pick a word you have trouble spelling.
2. Invent a trick line to remember the word.
3. Share it with your partner.
4. Talk quietly about your ideas.

Writing: Contractions

Strategy: Good writers use contractions.

1. Write a list of contractions.
2. Read them.
3. Write the missing words.
4. Talk quietly about your ideas.
5. Share these with the class.

Writing: Compound Words

Strategy: Good writers use compound words.

1 Write a list of compounds from your book.

2. Read them.

3. Draw a line between the two words.

4. Talk quietly about your ideas.

Writing: Abbreviations

Strategy: Good writers use abbreviations.

1. Write an abbreviation.

2. Have your partner write the word.

3. Repeat with other abbreviations.

4. Pick two to share with the class

Writing: Story Structure

Strategy: Good writers have an order to the story.

1. Read the story.
2. Think of the order of events of the story.
3. List these and write a sentence to go with each.
4. Share with the class.

At the beginning	
Then	
After this	
Then	
Finally	

Writing: E-mail Acronyms

Strategy: Good writers use ACRONYMS.

Sample Acronyms

BFN	**bye for now**
LOL	**laughing out loud**
TTYL	**talk to you later**

1. Write a list of acronyms.
2. Read them.
3. Write the missing words.
4. Talk quietly about your ideas.

Writing: Irregular Verb Forms

Strategy: Good writers use proper VERB forms.

Sample Irregular Verbs

am	**was**	**been**
are	**were**	**been**
bet	**bet**	**bet**
bite	**bit**	**bit**
blow	**blew**	**blown**

1. Write a present and past verb.
2. Write a sentence for each.
3. Talk quietly about your ideas.

Word-Play and Representing Strategies

We implement independent word-play and representing centres to further anchor our students' deeper conceptual word knowledge. We immerse students in either of these centres to once again situate them in the role of good readers and writers.

Word-play and representing centres give us good opportunities to differentiate the learning of ESL, at-risk, or low-progress students. New ESL learners in the intermediate grades can be working with the first words on the 100 Instant Word List (see "100 Instant Words" on page 129), while students with more language can access and track words systematically from words 75–100. Customized target vocabulary activities repeated a number of times provide at-risk or low-progress students with additional differentiated word-play activities that may be necessary to their vocabulary growth and development. We have a simple, practical means to manage a differentiated curriculum using the word-play and representing centres.

Good readers make sense of words through playing with words, specifically with onsets (the consonant preceding the vowel of a syllable) and rimes or phonograms (a vowel and any following consonant). This kind of phonemic awareness is not necessary for understanding spoken language but can be helpful for learning to read and write. Students in Grades 1 through 8 can have fun playing with words to improve their phonemic awareness and learn what how to be better readers and writers. There are many interesting ways to engage students in word play. The rest of this chapter provides some examples of strategies and activities that can be used to develop students' deeper conceptual understanding of many more words.

The strategies used at word-play or representing centres need to be modeled or taught to the whole group, so that students have a good working knowledge of them before they proceed to use them independently. These strategies can be modeled as mini-lessons at the conclusion of a read-aloud, during shared reading, or as a brief whole-class mini-lesson.

Word Play: Phonograms

Strategy: *Good readers look for patterns in words.*

Challenge students to play with many words by having them blend onsets, consonants, and rimes or phonograms to produce families of related words.

We develop their phonemic awareness of consonants, vowels, blending, segmentation, and rhyming with such challenges as

- identify the initial sound of a word, and then say and write the word with the initial sound deleted (e.g., pink→ ink)
- learn how to split rimes from the onsets (e.g., flab→lab)
- learn how to add a new onset to a rime or phonogram (e.g., /l/ + /ab/→lab)
- learn how to make word families from phonograms (e.g., ay → bay, day, hay, jay, lay, may, pay, ray)
- learn a connecting strategy: similar words can be used to solve unfamiliar words through analogy (e.g., knowing *at* helps with sat, mat, cat, rat)
- rearrange letters to make new words (e.g., stop→tops, spot→pots)

100 Instant Words

the	or	will	number
of	one	up	no
and	had	other	way
a	by	about	could
to	word	out	people
in	but	many	my
is	not	then	than
you	what	them	first
that	all	these	water
it	were	so	been
he	we	some	call
was	when	her	who
for	your	would	oil
on	can	make	its
are	said	like	now
as	there	him	find
with	use	into	long
his	an	time	down
they	each	has	day
I	which	look	did
at	she	two	get
be	do	more	come
this	know	write	made
have	their	go	may
from	if	see	part

A strong correlation has been found between the ability to perform these kinds of tasks and reading achievement through Grade 12.

Challenge students to play with the most common phonograms or less common ones, or to play with the phonograms of target words being anchored that day during the semantic mapping or shared reading. This is not simply isolated phonics instruction or practice but rather further training with the important words of the recurrent vocabulary instruction system. Primary students will typically play with phonograms in one- or two-syllable target words. Intermediate students work with the same phonograms appearing in targeted polysyllabic words.

Word Play: Fun with Phonograms

Strategies: Good readers play with words. Good readers look for patterns in words.

Challenge students to make lists of new words by adding letters, deleting letters, or mixing up letters in the words and phonograms provided (page 134). Another kind of challenge is to add, delete, or mix up letters from target or important words (page 135).

Word Play: Word Ladders

Strategy: Good readers can think of one word to know others in the same word family.

Changing the onset on a phonogram can build students' knowledge of other related words. Challenge students to find other words in the word families of their target or important words (page 136).

Word Play: Letter/Word Play

Strategies: Good readers look at one word to know about other words.
Good readers notice the letters at the beginning, middle, and end of a word.

Students can monitor their own progress of how many words they learn in a variety of different word families, especially those related to the target words being studied. They can keep track of which word families have the most members by using a point system. They can track their own progress on a class list. Peers, teaching assistants, or the teacher can assess them formally or informally on this word knowledge.

Challenge students to list all the words they know that start with the same letter as favorite or target words. Noticing and changing the final consonant can build students' knowledge of many words. Working with the middle sounds or letters of words challenges students' knowledge of words. Have students play with the beginning, medial, and final letters of their target words to ensure they have many passes at working with this important vocabulary (page 136). Students gain confidence as readers and writers as they learn to manipulate letters and sounds and become familiar with word patterns and families, especially when they see that they know many more words than they thought.

Word Play: Stand-alones

Strategy: Good readers know lots about words.

One example of word knowledge is the understanding that many words rhyme but some do not. Give students lists of words that are stand-alones, that don't rhyme, so they can begin to make sense of how some special kinds of words work. Students learn that some words do not have extensive word families and some have none at all. Working with these words challenges students to improve their metacognition of word knowledge by becoming familiar with how many different strategies are needed to make sense of the English language.

Word Play: Sight Words, Instant Words, and Frequently Used Words

Strategies: Good readers have a good store of sight words (eye-spelled words) or instant recognition words.
Good readers know how to read some words instantly.
Good readers know many frequently used words.

It is nearly impossible to write a sentence without the first 100 Instant Words (see "100 Instant Words" page 129). Fledgling readers have their work cut out for them. They must be able to recognize words easily and instantly so they don't spend all their time sounding them out, a tiring process if they want to get the text meaning. They need to learn both the instant recognition of these and the written form as well. With sight-word, instant-word, and frequently-used-word challenges, students learn that there are a number of different words that they need to know without word analysis, words that are just understood quickly and easily. Students come to know that many words cannot be sounded out and that they need to know these words instantly as a whole. They learn to check and see if these words look right. Students are able to make sense of these words as "eye-spelled" words, and of decoded words as "ear-spelled words." Many phonetically irregular and important common words are taught as sight words before the students have the skill to decode them.

> Just 100 words comprise half of all the words in *The New York Times,* half the words in the encyclopedia, and half of all the words in any children's book such as Grahame's book *The Wind in the Willows.* (Fry, 2001).

The Instant Words list shows that 100 most common words that make up 50% of all written material (see "100 Instant Words" on page 129). The first 300 words make up 65%, and the first 1,000 words make up over 90% of all written material (Fry, 2001).

Give students lists of sight words (page 137), instant words (page 138), and frequently used words (page 138) and challenge them to play with them, alone or in partners. Have them use a "look, say, write, and check" strategy to practise reading and writing these words. Give them opportunities to learn their important target words with this same strategy.

Word Play: Homophones, Synonyms, Homographs, and Antonyms

Strategy: Good readers know some words have different spellings and meanings.

Challenge students to play with looking, writing, and talking about lists of homophones (page 139), synonyms (page 139), homographs (page 140), and antonyms (page 140). Working in partners, they make and share their lists with the class to extend their individual and collective understanding of the meaning and structure of words.

Word Play: Non-Reversible Word Pairs

Students work with learning these special pairings of words by making lists of them and challenging their peers to discover the ones that are not in the correct order (page 141). This centre provides readers and writers with further knowledge of the nuances of spoken language. Students enjoy discovering their own non-reversible word pairs with family and friends. This kind of word play gets students thinking and talking about their word knowledge.

Word Play: Making a Word Search

Challenge students to create a word search (page 141) using target or important words that are being anchored, for a partner to do. They can refer to the semantic map that has been constructed during the read-aloud or shared reading text. This challenge gives students another pass at anchoring the words that have been previously introduced and worked with. It gives them an opportunity to play with the same words many times. They will be looking at the words, listing the words, and adding them to the word search. When they do the word search their partner has made for them, they will be playing with them again. When they check each other's word search, they are provided with yet another pass to anchor this vocabulary.

Word Play: Greek and Latin Roots for Words

Challenge students to learn about a variety of Greek and Latin words (pages 142, 143) to assist them when they come across new words that may have such origins. Once they have some working knowledge of the origins of words or roots, they can be challenged to determine such origins when they come across new target or personal interest words. The knowledge of the origin of words and their associated meanings extends students' knowledge to many words they will read and write.

Word Play: Similes

Challenge students to read and write some similes (page 144) to reinforce this important strategy for both reading and writing.

Word Play: What Do You Notice? and Listen and Sketch Stories

Challenge students to make pictures to go with some of the vocabulary they have been working with during shared reading (page 145). Have them take some time to think about the words around their target word. Have them represent their learning with illustrations of the multiple meanings of their chosen words. Challenge students to draw the target words of a story as they listen to it while one member of the group rereads it during the centre (page 145). Have the students share their drawings with the class at the closing of centre time.

Word Play: Clip-art and 3-D Representing

Strategy : Good readers and writers notice the multiple meanings of words.

Challenge students to search for clip art to represent their understanding of the meanings of target words (page 146). Have them search the Internet as a source for new information on their words. Engaging in searches for new meanings is part of being a good reader.

Challenge students to make three-dimensional representations of their learning to extend their deep concept knowledge of the words. They can work with building systems, junk (imagination market items), or clay to represent their understanding of the meanings of words. Have students from other centres make predictions of what target words the students have represented.

Word Play: Build a Good Sentence

Strategy : Good readers and writers think carefully about their words to show rather than tell the story.

Challenge students to create good sentences by scaffolding the process with a Who, What, Why, When, and Where grid for the construction of good sentences. Challenge your students to create their own grid to go with the read-aloud or shared reading activity of the day and target words (page 146). This opportunity to play with constructing good sentences and share them with the class engages their metacognition about careful word usage. Students may choose to work in partners to construct their sentences.

Word Play: Word Chunks

Strategy : Good readers and writers chunk word parts.

Challenge students to use a chunking strategy to work with big words (page 147). Have students select large words from a picture dictionary and work to chunk them so they can say them. Help students develop tenacity in learning how to say, write, explain, and use big words. Develop their confidence to use all the strategies they are learning to reinforce their abilities to fearlessly attack large words.

Word Play: Phonograms

Strategy: Good readers look for patterns in words.

Sample

at →b<u>at</u>, c<u>at</u>, f<u>at</u>, h<u>at</u>, m<u>at</u>, gn<u>at</u>, p<u>at</u>, r<u>at</u>, s<u>at</u>, v<u>at</u>

1. Choose your favorite phonogram from this list.

-ay	-ick	-eed	-ink	-ake
-ill	-ell	-y	-ow	-ine
-ip	-ot	-out	-ew	-ight
-at	-ing	-ug	-ore	-im
-am	-ap	-op	-ed	-um
-ag	-unk	-in	-ab	
-ack	-ail	-an	-ob	
-ank	-ain	-est	-ock	

2. Make a list of words containing the phonogram to share with the class.

3. Put a colored line under the pattern.

Word Play: Phonograms

Strategy: Good readers look for patterns in words.

Sample
target word: parade
phonogram: /ade → b⟦ade⟧, bl⟦ade⟧, f⟦ade⟧, j⟦ade⟧, m⟦ade⟧, w⟦ade⟧

1. Look at one of your important target words. Figure out the phonogram in the word.

2. Make a list of other words containing the same phonogram to share with the class.

3. Put a colored box around the pattern.

Word Play: Fun With Phonograms

Strategy: Good readers play with words.
Good readers look for patterns in words.

1. Look at your target or important words.

2. Make 3 lists of new words.

   List 1: Words with letters added to a target word.

   List 2: Words with letters mixed up in the target word.

   List 3: Words with letters left out of the target word.

3. Share these lists with the class.

Word Play: Word Ladders

Strategy: Good readers can think of one word to know other words in the same family.

Sample Strategy

   If you know *black* you know sack, pack, rack, stack, back, hack, jack, and lack.

1. Choose your important target words.

_____

_____

2. Write all the words you know in one word family of one of your target words.

3. Get ten points for every correctly spelled word.

Word Play: Letter/Word Play

1. Look at your important target words.

2. Write all the words you know that are the same at

Strategy: Good readers can look at one word to know if the other word is almost the same. Good readers notice the letters at the beginning, the middle, and the end of words.

• the beginning of the word

• the middle of the word

• the end of the word

3. Get ten points for every correctly spelled word.

Word Play: Stand-alones

Strategy: Good readers know some words don't rhyme.

Sample Words

bulb, silver, exit, orange, film, purple, wasp, zebra, noisy, hundred, dreamt

1. Make a list for the class of words that don't rhyme.
2. Look at a word from the list.
3. Say the word.
4. Write the word.
5. Check the word.
6. Close your eyes and picture each word in your mind.
7. Find some other words that do not rhyme.

Word Play: Sight Words (eye-spelled words)

Strategy: Good readers look to see if they instantly know a word and the word looks right (eye-spelled). You *cannot* sound out all words (ear-spelled).

1. Choose your favorite eye-spelled sight words; for example,
   again, any, become, been, both, bread, brought, climbed, come, could, country, design, do, does, earth, enough, eyes, father, four, friends, give, group, heard, island, learn, listen, may measure, mountain, move, off, of, often, once, one, other, people, piece, said, science, should, sign, something, should, stretch, the, their, they, thought, to, two, want, was, watch, were, who, women, world, you, young, youth
2. Look at the word. Do not sound it out.
3. Say the word.
4. Write the word.
5. Read the word fast. Say the word fast.
6. Close your eyes and picture the wacky word in your mind.

Word Play: Instant Words

Strategy: Good readers know many words **instantly**.

1. Look at the list of 100 First Words.
2. Begin with the first word on the list.
3. Look at the word.
4. Say the word.
5. Write the word.
6. Check the word.
7. Close your eyes and picture the word in your mind.
8. Go onto the next word and do the same.

Word Play: Frequently Used Words

Strategy: Good readers know many **frequently used** words.

Frequently Used Words

a, after, all, am, an, and, are, as, asked, at, away, back, be, because, before, big, boy, but, by, came, can, come, could, day, did, do, don't, down, for, food, from, get, go, going, had, has, have, he, her, here, him, his, house, how, I, I'm, if, in, into, is, it, just, keep, kind, know, like, little, long, look, make, man, mother, me, my, no, not, now, of, old, on, one, or, our, out, over, people, play, put, ran, run, said saw, see

1. Look at each word.
2. Say the word.
3. Write the word.
4. Check the word.
5. Close your eyes and picture the word in your mind.

Word Play: Homophones

Strategy: Good readers know some words have different spellings and meanings.

Sample Homophones

Ad, add	ant, aunt	be, bee	blue, blue	dear, deer
beat, beet	cell, sell	cellar, seller	cent, scent	feat, feet
By, bye, buy	I, eye, aye	or, ore, oar	fir, fur	hair, hare
heal, heel	hi, high	hay, her	hear, here	hall, haul

1. List one homophone.
2. Have a partner write the matching word (look on the list above if you need help).
3. Look at the words.
4. Say the words.
5. Talk about how the words are spelled. Talk about what the words mean.
6. Close your eyes and picture both words in your mind.

Word Play: Synonyms

Strategy: Good readers and writers know many words for one word.

Sample Synonyms

small – little – tiny	back – rear – behind
boy – lad – youth	girl – gal

1. List one synonym.
2. Have a partner write a matching synonym.
3. Write another matching synonym.
4. Look at the words.
5. Say the words together.
6. Talk about how the words are different.

Word Play: Homographs

Sample Homographs

bat (animal) – bat (in baseball)   jam (fruit spread) – jam (to force together)

slug (hit) – slug (snail)   heel (on your foot) – heel (to walk beside)

lap (made when you sit) – lap (to lick at) – lap (one phase of a race)

1. Write a homograph.
2. Have a partner write the matching homograph.
3. Look at the words.
4. Say the words.
5. Talk about how the word meanings are different.
6. Close your eyes and picture the words.
7. Act out some of these words.

Word Play: Antonyms

Sample Antonyms

above – below   black – white

bad – good   high – low

1. List one antonym.
2. Have a partner write the opposite word.
3. Look at the words.
4. Say the words.
5. Talk about how the words are different.
6. Close your eyes and picture the words in your mind.

Word Play: Non-reversible Word Pairs

Strategy: Good writers know that many words are said in a special order.

Sample Non-reversible Word Pairs

bacon and eggs, fish and chips, bride and groom, cup and saucer, dead or alive, front and centre, ham and eggs, knife and fork, life and death, lost and found, man and wife, name and address, pen and pencil, rain or shine, salt and pepper, sooner or later, sweet and sour, tall and thin, up and down

1. Choose the words you like.

2. Make a list of three word pairs.

3. Switch the words in one pair so they are in the *wrong* order.

4. See if others can guess which pair is in the wrong order.

Word Play: Making a Word Search

Strategy: Good readers know about the structure of words.

To make a WORD SEARCH for your partner:

1. Make a list of important words from the semantic map.

2. Put the words neatly on grid paper.

3. Add other letters in the empty squares around the words to fill in each box in the grid.

4. Trade word searches with your partners.

Word Play: Greek Root Words

Strategy: Good readers know that many words come from Greek root words.

Greek Root	Meaning	Words with Root
ast	star	asteroid
bio	life	biology
cosm	universe	cosmos
cycl	circle	cycle
gen	birth	generation
geo	earth	geography
gram	letter writing	telegram
graph	write	autograph
meter	measure	centimeter
path	feeling	empathy
phon	sound	telephone
photo	light	photogenic
saur	lizard	dinosaur

1. Pick a Greek root. Print the meaning beside it.

2. Find or think of other words with this Greek root.

3. Close your eyes and picture the word. Write it.

4. Find other Greek roots and words.

Word Play: Latin Root Words

Strategy: Good readers know that many words come from Latin root words.

Latin Root	Meaning	Words with Root
act	do	act
anim	life	animal
ann	year	annual
aqua	water	aquatic
aud	hear	audio
card	heart	cardiac
corp	body	corpse
duc	lead	educate
form	shape	uniform
loc	place	locate
mob, mot	shape	motion
mort	dead	mortal
ped	foot	pedal
port	carry	portable
sign	mark	signal
tract	pull	tractor
vac	empty	vacuum
vid, vis	see	visor
volve	turn	revolve

1. Pick a Latin root. Print the meaning beside it.

2. Find or think of other words with this Latin root.

3. Close your eyes and picture the word. Write it.

4. Find other Latin roots and words.

Word Play: Similes

Strategies: Good readers make pictures in their minds from the words they read.
Good writers use similes — *as* and *like* — to put pictures in a reader's mind.

Sample Similes

as soft as a pillow	cry like a baby
as bright as . . .	chatter like a . . .
as clear as . . .	cry like a . . .
as cold as . . .	eats like a . . .
as cool as. . .	fits like a . . .
as deep as . . .	laughs like a. . .
as fat as . . .	run like a . . .
as flat as . . .	slept like a . . .
as happy as . . .	sparkled like a. . .
as hungry as . . .	walked like a . . .
as loud as . . .	worked like a . . .
as lovely as . . .	moves like a . . .
as quick as . . .	fought like a . . .
as rough as . . .	sit like a . . .
as slow as . . .	yelled like a . . .
as smart as . . .	waddled like a . . .

1. Read the list of similes. Pick some you like.

2. Write your own similes.

3. Close your eyes and picture the words in your mind.

4. Read these to the class. Ask them to make pictures in their minds of the similes you share.

Word Play: What Do You Notice?

Strategy: Good readers and writers make pictures in their minds.

1. Choose an interesting word from the shared reading.

2. Why did you notice it?

3. Look at the words AROUND IT.

4. What other meaning does it have?

5. Try to draw several meanings of the word.

Word:	Word:
Meaning/ Picture	Meaning/ Picture

Word Play: Listen and Sketch Stories

Strategy: Good readers picture the story.

1. Listen for the target words in a read aloud.

2. Draw the words while you listen to it.

3. Share your drawings with the class.

Word Play: Clip-art and 3-D Representing

Strategy: Good readers and writers notice the multiple meanings of words. Good readers find new word meanings by asking or looking.

1. Search for clip art to match the meanings of your 4 to 6 new words. Or find blocks, junk, and play clay.
2. Import and label the pictures, or build models of the images of your words.
3. Share your pictures and models with the class.

Word Play: Build a Good Sentence

Strategy: Good readers and writers think carefully about their words to show rather than tell the story.

Words from the Read-aloud Semantic Map

Who?	What?	Why?	When?	Where?
boy	swam	for fun	at dawn	on an island

1. Make a lists of words to go with the read-aloud.
2. Pick a word from each list to make a GOOD sentence.
3. Look at the words.
4. Say the words.
5. Close your eyes and picture the words.
6. Write a good sentence to go with the story using your words.

Who	What	Why	When	Where

Word Play: Word Chunks

Strategy: Good readers and writers CHUNK WORD PARTS.

Sample

Tikkitikkitembo-nosarembo-charibariruchi-pipperipembo is the name of a little boy in the book *Tikki Tikki Tembo* retold by Arlene Mosel (1968).

1. Write some BIG words from the picture dictionary.
2. Have your partner chunk each word by putting spaces between the word parts.
3. Pick two to share with the class. Share the *meaning* of the words as well.

Conclusion

I asked the new little boy with the undecidedly brown hair what his favorite word was.

"*It*," he replied after a thoughtful pause. I asked him why this was his favorite word.

He shrugged his shoulders and said he really didn't even know if he liked words, but that *it* didn't give him any trouble like the others!

Learning to read and write is a difficult and distasteful task for many students. Despite reams of research on impressive, sweeping changes in methods and materials for vocabulary instruction, we have not yet met the needs of producing a functionally literate generation.

So the challenge is set for every elementary school teacher. How do we create a learning environment that is favorable for the study of our beautiful, complex collection of words? How can we make an environment that encourages and rewards the exploration of print by every child — especially our little boys with undecidedly brown hair? How do we even begin to make sense of our time together as a totally meaningful and memorable event that sticks in the minds of our young students?

I myself could not even imagine not loving words. I have loved words since I could remember. I can still recall the enchanting sound of "Rikki Tikki Tavi" as it rolled off my father's lips as he read to me. I can recollect the delightful sound of "Chicka Chicka Boom Boom, Will there be enough room . . . " (Bill Martin, Jr.) as it rolled off my lips as I read to my Grade 1 class.

I have discovered that words are wonderful and fun and can stick for a lifetime. I have also discovered that words can be just as wonderful and fun for our students and can stick for their lifetimes too.

I have also come to realize that what actually, and totally, makes words stick is the interest and delight in them, that we pass down to our children.

Words stick when we
- share a wide range of materials worthy of our students' attention and interest
- present read-alouds and picture studies with heart and soul that serve the life interests of our students
- take the time to share our most prized stories and have our students share theirs
- have a ritual to talk about which stories we adore and why we adore them
- give our students situational support of read-alouds and picture studies to do justice to the nuances of the language
- give students practice with words first in the context of a story rather than in isolation
- give students exposure to a wide variety of types of print
- give students prior knowledge of a topic to help them make sense of a passage before they read it

- just read a book, nothing more
- fuss over a book, and do lots more
- give students independent practice time

Words stick when the students
- are given social support and active learning opportunities without any sense of competition
- work collaboratively to make sense/purpose of print and the pleasures of print
- work independently at their level and pace with some choice of material
- are taught strategies for self-correction and evaluation from the beginning
- develop positive attitudes and skills to be good readers and writers
- have choice of what to read and who to read with
- learn to think a word is important enough to make it mean something
- are taught in an enjoyable environment where the study of words is an adventure
- read extensively in age-appropriate books

Making words stick is not about how much vocabulary we can teach them, but how much love we can put into the teaching and learning of it.

After several months working with my little brown-haired boy, I asked him the question again. What's your favorite word?

"Tikki Tikki Tembo–no sa rembo–charibariruchi–pipperi pembo," he smiled.

I smiled back.

Bibliography

Allen, J. (1999). *Words, Words, Words*. Portland, ME. Stenhouse Publishers.

Allington, R. & Cunningham, P. (1999). *Classrooms That Work*. New York: Addison-Wesley Longman.

Anderson, R.C. Hiebert, E.H., Scott, J.A. & Wilkinson, I.A.G. (1985). *Becoming a Nation of Readers: The Report of the Commission on Reading*. Washington, DC: National Institute of Education.

Anderson, R. & Nagy, W. (1991). "Word Meanings" 690–724 in R. Barr, M. Kamala, P. Monsenthal & P.D. Pearson, eds., *Handbook of Reading Research*, Vol. 2. Mahwah, NJ: Lawrence Erlbaum Associates.

Atwell, N. (1987). *In the Middle: Writing, Reading and Learning with Adolescents*. Portsmouth, NH: Boynton Cook Publishers.

Baker, S.K., Simmons, D.C. & Kameenui, E. J. (1995a). *Vocabulary Acquisition: Curricular and Instructional Implications For Diverse Learners*. University of Oregon: National Centre to Improve the Tools for Educators.

Baker, S.K., Simmons, D.C. & Kameenui, E. J. (1995b). *Vocabulary Acquisition: Curricular and Instructional Implications For Diverse Learners*. University of Oregon: National Centre to Improve the Tools for Educators.

Banikowski, A.K. & Mehring, T.A. (1999). "Strategies to Enhance Memory Based Brain Research" *Focus on Exceptional Children*, 32 (2), 1–16.

Baumann, J. F. & Kameenui, E.J. (1991). "Research on Vocabulary Instruction: Ode to Voltaire" 604–32 in J. Flood, J.M. Jensen, D. Lapp & J.R. Squire, eds., *Handbook of Research on Teaching the English Language Arts*. New York: Macmillan.

Beck, I.L., McKeown, M.G. & Kucan, I. (2002). *Bringing Words to Life: Robust Vocabulary Instruction*. New York: Guilford.

Beck, I.L., Perfetti, C.A. & McKeown, M.G. (1982). "The Effects of Long-term Vocabulary Instruction on Lexical Access and Reading Comprehension" *Journal of Educational Psychology*, 74, 506–21.

Biemiller, A. (2001). "Teaching Vocabulary" *American Educator*, Spring, 143–148.

Blachowicz, C.L.Z., & Fisher, P. (2004). "Vocabulary Lessons" *Education Leadership*, Vol. 61, No. 6, 66–69.

Booth, D. (2001). *Reading and Writing in the Middle Years*. Marhkam, ON: Pembroke Publishers.

Brassel, D. & Flood, J. (2004). *Vocabulary Strategies Every Teacher Needs to Know*. San Diego, CA: Academic Professional Development.

Bryant, D.P., Ugel, N., Thompson, S. & Hamff, A. (1999). "Instructional Strategies for Content-area Reading Instruction" *Intervention in School and Clinic*, 34 (5), 293–302.

Buehl, D. (1997). "Loud and Clear" *The Reading Room*[Online]. Available: http: www.weac.org/News/SEPT97/read.htm.

Buis, K. (2002). *The Daily Letter: Redefining, Reconceptualizing and Reconditioning Genre in the Elementary Classroom*. Vancouver, BC: Simon Fraser University.

Buis, K. (2004). *Writing Everyday*. Markham, ON: Pembroke Publishers.

Caine, R. & Caine, G. (1994). *Making Connections: Teaching and the Human Brain*. Reading, MA: Addison-Wesley.

Calhoun, E.F. (1999). *Teaching Beginning Reading and Writing with the Picture Word Inductive Method*. Alexandria, VA: ASCD.

Calkins, Lucy McCormick. (1986). *The Art of Teaching Writing*. Portsmouth, NH: Heinemann.

Calkins, Lucy McCormick. (1991). *Living Between the Lines*. Portsmouth, NH: Heinemann.

Calkins, Lucy McCormick. (1994). *The Art of Teaching Writing*, New edition. Portsmouth, NH: Heinemann.

Cambourne, B., Fitzsimmon, P. & Geekie, P. (1999). *Understanding Literacy Development*. Stoke on Trent, UK: Trentham Books.

Chambers, A. (1991). *The Reading Environment*. Portland, ME: Stenhouse Publishers.

Chapman, M. L. (1997). *Webs of Meaning: Writing in the Elementary School*. Toronto, ON: ITP Nelson.

Chapman, M.L. (1999). "Situated, Social Active Learning Rewriting Genre in the Elementary Classroom." *Communications*, Vol. 16, No. 4, 469–90.

Clay, M. (1985). *The Early Detection of Reading Difficulties*, 3rd edition. Portsmouth, NH: Heinemann.

Clay, M. (1991). *Becoming Literate: The Construction of Inner Control*. Portsmouth, NH: Heinemann.

Clay, M. (1993). *An Observation Survey of Early Literacy Achievement*. Portsmouth, NH: Heinemann.

Cunningham, A. & Stanovich, K. (1997). "Early Reading Acquisition and its Relation to Reading Experience and Ability 10 years later" *Developmental Psychology*, 33, 934–45.

Cunningham, A. & Stanovich, K. (1998). "What Reading Does for the Mind" *American Educator*, Spring/Summer), 8–15.

Deffes, R. & Juel, C. (2004). "Making Words Stick" *Educational Leadership*, Vol. 61, No. 6, 30–34.

Eeds, M. & Wells, D. (1989). "Grand Conversations: An Exploration of meaning construction and understanding in literature study groups" *Research in the Teaching of English*, 23(1), 4–29.

Ehri, L.C. & Robbins, C. (1992). "Beginners need some decoding skills to read words by analogy" *Reading Research Quarterly*, 27, 13–26.

Ehri, L.C. (2000). "Learning to read and learning to spell: two sides of a coin" *Topics in Language Disorders*, 20(3), 19–36.

Flippo, R.F. (2001). *Reading Researchers in Search of Common Ground*. Newark, DE: International Reading Association.

Fry, Kress & Fountoukidis. (2000). *The Reading Teacher's Book of Lists*. NJ: Prentice Hall.

Fu, D. & Townsend, J. (1999). "Serious Learning: Language Lost" *Language Arts*, 76(5) 404–11.

Goodland, J. (1984). *A Place Called School. Prospects for the future*. New York: McGraw Hill.

Goodman,Y.M. & Wilde, S. (1996). *Notes From a Kidwatcher: Selected Writings of Yetta M. Goodman*. Portsmouth, NH: Heinemann.

Goodman, K.S. (1978). "Kidwatching: An alternative to testing" *National Elementary School Principal*, 57, 41–45.

Goodman, K.S. (1985). "Kidwatching: Observing Children in the Classroom" 9–18 in A. Jaggar and M.T. Smith-Burke (Eds.), *Observing the Language Learner*. Newark, DE: IRA and Urbana, IL: National Council of Teachers of English.

Graves, D. (1983). *Writing: Teachers and Children at Work*. Portsmouth, NH: Heinemann.

Graves, M. (2000). "A Vocabulary Program to Complement and Bolster a Middle-Grade Comprehension Program" 116–135 in B. Taylor, M. Graves & P. can den Brock (Eds,), *Reading for Meaning: Fostering Comprehension in the Middle Grades*. Newark, DE: International Reading Association.

Graves, M. & Watts-Taffe, S. (2002). "The Place of Word Consciousness in a Research Based Vocabulary Reading Program" 140–65 in A. Farstrup & S.J. Samuels (Eds,·) *What Research has to Say About Reading Instruction*, 3rd edition. Newark, DE: International Reading Assocaition.

Guthrie, J. T. & Wigfield, A. (1997). *Reading Engagement. Motivating Readers Through Integrated Instruction*. Newark. DE. International Reading Association.

Guthrie, J.T. & Wigfield, A. (1999). "Engagement and Motivation in Reading" *Handbook of Reading Research*, Vol. III, 403–422.

Holdaway, D. (1974). *Independence in Reading*. Auckland, NZ: Ashton Scholastic.

Holdaway, D. (1979). *The Foundations of Literacy*. Auckland, NZ: Ashton Scholastic.

Krashen, S. (1993). *The Power of Reading*. Englewood, CO: Libraries Unlimited Inc.

Mamchure, C. (1997). *Designs for Learning: Writing. Education 485 Study Guide. Faculty of Education and Centre for Distance Education*. Vancouver, BC: Simon Fraser University.

Mamchure, C. (1990). "But. . . the Curriculum" *Phi Delta Kappan*, 71(8), 634–7.

Moats, L. (2001). "Overcoming the Language Gap" *American Educator*, Spring, 5–9.

Mooney, M. (1990). *Reading to, with and by Children*. Katonah, NY: Richard C. Owen.

Murray, D. (1968). *A Writer Teaches Writing: A Practical Method of Teaching Composition*. Boston, MA: Houghton Mifflin.

Nagy, W., Anderson, R.C. & Herman, R. (1985). "Learning Words From Context" *Reading Research Quarterly*, Winter, 233–53.

Nagy, W. & Herman, P.A. (1987). "Depth and Breadth of Vocabulary Knowledge: Implications for Acquisition and Instruction" 24–56 in M.C. McKeown & M. E. Curtis(Eds.). *The Nature of Vocabulary Acquisition*. Hilldale, NJ: Earlbaum.

Nagy, W. (1988). *Teaching Vocabulary to Improve Reading Comprehension*. Newark, DE: International Reading Association.

Nagy, W. & Scott, J. (2000). "Vocabulary Processes" 269–84 in M.L. Kamil, P. Mosenthal, P.D. Pearson, and R. Barr (Eds.), *Handbook of Reading Research*, Vol.III. Mahwah, NJ: Lawrence Erlbaum Associates.

National Reading Panel. (2000). *Teaching Children to Read: An Evidence-Based Assessment of the Scientific Research Literature on Reading and its Implications for Reading Instruction*. Washington, DC: National Institute of Child and Health and Human Development.

Popp, M.S. (1996). *Teaching Language and Literature in Elementary Classrooms*. Mahwah, NJ: Lawrence Erlbaum Associates.

Raphael, T.E. (1982). "Question-Answering Strategies for Children" *The Reading Teacher*, 36, 186–90.

Rosenblatt, L. (1937, 1978). *Literature as Exploration*. New York: D.L. Appleton, Century.

Rosenblatt, L. (1978). *The Teacher, the Text and the Poem: the Transactional Theory of the Literacy Work*. IL: Southern Illinois Press.

Ruddell, R. B., Unrau, M.R. & Singer, H. (1994). "Reading as a Meaning Construction Process: The Reader the Text and the Teacher" *Theoretical Models and Processes of Reading*, 4th edition. Newark, DE: International Reading Association.

Rogoff, B. (1990). *Apprenticeship in Thinking: Cognitive Development in Social Contexts*. New York: Oxford University Press.

Rogoff, B., Matusov, E. E. & White, C. (1996). "Models for Teaching and Learning: Participation in a Community of Learners" in Olson, D. & Torrance, N. *The Handbook of Education and Human Development: New Models of Learning, Teaching and Schooling*. Cambridge, MA.: Blackwell.

Sadler, C. (2001). *Comprehension Strategies for Middle Grade Learners: A Handbook for Content Area Teachers*. Newark, DE: International Reading Association.

Santa, C.M. (1990). "Teaching as Research" in *Opening the Door to Classroom Research*, Mary W. Olson (Ed). Newark, DE: International Reading Association.

Scala, M. (2001). *Working Together Reading and Writing in Inclusive Classrooms.* Newark, DE: International Reading Association.

Schwartz, S. & Bone, M. (1995). *Retelling, Relating and Reflecting.* Toronto, ON: Irwin.

Scott, J., Jamieson, N. D. & Asselin, M. (2003). "Vocabulary Instruction Throughout the School Day in 23 Canadian Upper-Elementary Classrooms" *The Elementary School Journal,* 103 (3), 269–86.

Short, K. & Pierce, K. K. (1990). *Talking About Books: Creating Literate Communities.* Toronto, ON: Irwin Publishing.

Vacca, R.T. & Vacca, J.L. (1989). *Content Area Reading,* 3rd ed. New York: HarperCollins.

Wells, G. (1986). *The Meaning Makers, Children Learning Language and Using Language to Learn.* Portsmouth, NH: Heinneman.

Wells, G. (1999). *Dialogic Inquiry Towards a Socio-Cultural Practice and Theory of Education.* Cambridge, UK: Cambridge University Press.

Wells, G. & Chang-Wells, G. (1992). *Constructing Knowledge Together: Classrooms as Centres of Inquiry and Literacy.* Portsmouth, NH: Heinemann.

Wlodkowski, R. (1985). *Enhancing Adult Motivation to Learn.* San Francisco, CA: Jossey Bass.

Children's Books Cited

Martin Jr., B. (1989). *Chicka Chicka Boom Boom.* New York: Simon and Schuster.

Mosel, A. (1968). *Tikki Tikki Tembo.* New York: Holt, Rinehart and Winston.

Rylant, C. (1998). *Scarecrow.* New York: Harcourt Brace Children's Books.

White, E. B. (1997). *Charlotte's Web.* New York: Harper and Row.

Index